10659887

PHILOSOPHY

PHILOSOPHY

FROM THE ANCIENT GREEKS TO GREAT THINKERS OF MODERN TIMES

ANNE ROONEY

Picture Credits

Bridgeman Images: 41 (Private Collection), 71 (Yale Center for British Art, Paul Mellow Collection, USA), 81 (Hamburger Kunsthalle, Hamburg, Germany), 96 (Private Collection/photo © Christie's Images)
Corbis: 29 (adoc-photos), 94 (Bettmann), 112 (Heritage Images), 203 (Alfredo Dagli Orti/The Art Archive), 216 (Stapleton Collection), 224 (Christel Gerstenberg), 235 (Bettmann)
Getty Images: 182, 239 (2011 Sven Loach)
Kobal Collection: 15 (Paramount/Melinda Sue Gordon), 23 (Prana-Film)
Mary Evans Picture Library: 178, 180 (BILL), 226 (Peter Higginbotham Collection)
Science Photo Library: 129 (Mehau Kulyk)

This edition published in 2020 by Arcturus Publishing Limited
26/27 Bickels Yard, 151–153 Bermondsey Street,
London SE1 3HA

Copyright © Arcturus Holdings Limited

All rights reserved. No part of this publication may be reproduced, stored in a retrieval system, or transmitted, in any form or by any means, electronic, mechanical, photocopying, recording or otherwise, without prior written permission in accordance with the provisions of the Copyright Act 1956 (as amended). Any person or persons who do any unauthorised act in relation to this publication may be liable to criminal prosecution and civil claims for damages.

AD006718UK

Printed in the UK

Contents

INTRODUCTION
The examined life

---

*'What I really lack is to be clear in my mind what
I am to do . . . the thing is to find a truth which
is true for me, to find the idea for which I can live and die.'*
Søren Kierkegaard, *Journals* (1836)

Finding 'the truth which is true for me': this is the business
of philosophy. It is not a luxury, an abstruse pursuit for those

with the time to sit in an ivory tower. It is a tool by which humans can work out how to live, how to endure misfortune, how to think about the world around them and how to relate to others.

It is essentially asking questions – the biggest questions imaginable. Philosophers have asked questions such as: 'What is reality?' 'Does God exist?' 'How can we know if something is true?' 'What is virtue?' and 'Is what is "right" or "wrong" the same for all people, places and times?'

Does it matter?

You might feel that you can get through life without deciding what reality is, but you will still stumble over philosophy in the questions that crop up for all thinking people in everyday life:

- Do animals have rights?
- Should we allow terminally sick people to die when they choose to?
- If social deprivation pushes someone into crime, should they be punished?
- Does it matter if you avoid paying tax?
- Do people have a right to say things that upset others?

Philosophy provides us with a framework and a toolkit for tackling such questions.

ASKING QUESTIONS

This book addresses some of the questions and some of the attempts made to answer them over the 2,500-year history of Western philosophy. Philosophical questions are not susceptible to a single, correct or 'true' answer. Trying to answer them is a task beset with difficulties, not least because philosophers don't agree on what constitutes 'truth', what it means to 'know' anything, or even the status of the words we use to express the questions and answers.

> *'The unexamined life is not worth living.'*
> Socrates as quoted by Plato (*c.*427–347BC)

> *'I doubt, therefore I think, therefore I am.'*
> René Descartes, *The Discourse on the Method* (1637)

In discussing the deep questions that can help us to find 'the idea for which I can live and die', we are continuing a dialogue that began with the Ancient Greek philosopher Socrates (470–399BC) and is unlikely ever to end. As time passes, the world we live in changes and the parameters of the debate shift. Although the world we live in today is very different from the one that Socrates knew, the questions we ask are very similar. We still seek to live a virtuous life, ask whether or not there is a God, and strive to know what is true about the world around us. But advances in scientific knowledge, exposure to very different societies and cultures around the world, and shifting social structures have changed the direction of the debate.

In the same way that modern Christians, Jews, Muslims and Hindus have a firm conviction that their gods exist, the Ancient Greeks believed that gods such as Zeus, Poseidon and Aphrodite were real.

The whole can of worms

'There is nothing.
If there were anything, no one would know it.
If anyone did know it, no one could communicate it.'

This bleak view of the meaninglessness of existence by the Ancient Greek philosopher Gorgias (*c*.483–375BC) makes philosophy look a pretty barren and hopeless endeavour. But it's a starting point, and one that the French philosopher René Descartes was to use 2,000 years later when he set out to determine what, if anything, exists and how we can be sure of it. Before we start to look at how philosophers have approached the question of existence, we will pause to think about 'being' and 'knowing', as the two – though treated separately hereafter – are impossible to separate fully.

Being and knowing

Which of the following do you believe exists?

- Yourself
- The last person you spoke to
- The clothes you are wearing

If you trust the evidence of your senses and your memory, and you trust in the continued existence of something after it has passed out of your sight, you will believe all of these exist.

Even to the casual enquirer, though, the existence of some things is clearly not certain. Here are some things you probably haven't seen. Which, if any, of the following do you believe exists?

- Narwhals
- Atoms
- Yetis

- God
- Fairies

Most people believe things told to them by sources they consider authoritative. You probably believe I exist, as someone must have written the book and if it was not the 'I' that is named on the cover it would be an 'I' that is someone else.

Plenty of people have seen narwhals even if you haven't – you can see videos of them on YouTube, and read about their biology. It would take a massive conspiracy for some group to have invented narwhals and then kept the deception going for centuries. Indeed, it's simpler for them to exist than not exist (but that in itself is not evidence of their existence).

> **SPOTLIGHT ON PHILOSOPHERS**
> *The Greek philosopher Aristotle (384–322BC) would say we certainly have enough evidence to agree that narwhals exist.*
> *The Anglo-Irish philosopher George Berkeley (1685–1753) would say that even seeing a narwhal yourself doesn't give you irrefutable evidence of their existence.*

Most people believe established science gives an accurate account of the world. We haven't seen atoms, but there is plenty of evidence to support their existence. They make sense.

There are signs that might be evidence of yetis, but those signs could have been misinterpreted. No one has indisputably seen yetis. As they would be visible if they existed, this casts doubt on their existence – but it doesn't prove there are no yetis.

What about God? Some people are so devout that they believe the existence of God is as likely as their own existence. Others, however, deny there is a God at all. Far fewer people believe in fairies – but some do, and more used to. There is no more solid physical evidence for the existence of God than there is for the existence of fairies. Here we have another source of 'evidence' – personal conviction or instinct. Sometimes, a firmly held belief is more convincing to an individual than the evidence of science or reason.

IT'S TRUE IF WE BELIEVE IT'S TRUE!

'Consensus reality' is socially constructed reality. If enough people believe something exists it is treated as reality. Throughout history, people who rejected the consensus reality have been ridiculed, ostracized, treated as mad or criminally minded, exiled and even put to death. In a strict religious community in particular, the consensus reality is that God exists. Anyone who does not share the predominant conception of God is likely to be persecuted.

Let's make the question a bit trickier. Which of these do you believe exists?

- A conversation you had last week
- Justice
- The hole in a doughnut
- A poem you have made up in your head, but not written down or spoken aloud

Now we are in the realm of things that logically we have to say don't exist, yet we may believe that they do have some kind of existence. We've run up against the problem of what we mean by 'exist' – both what it is to 'be' and what the word 'exist' means to us.

A conversation you had last week caused vibrations in the air that have now dissipated. It produced chemical and electrical changes in your brain, and the brain of other participants, which have now gone. Yet it exists in your memory and in those of others present at the time.

'Justice' has no physical existence. It exists purely as a concept in the minds of people and as enshrined in laws. There is no universal agreement about what constitutes justice.

SPOTLIGHT ON PHILOSOPHERS

Plato would say that there is an ideal form of justice, which all human attempts at realizing justice strive towards but never attain.

The French writer Michel de Montaigne (1533–92) would say that justice is different in different societies and no one version is better than another in absolute terms.

The hole in a ring doughnut is an absence of doughnut rather than part of the doughnut itself, an area of 'not-doughnut', as it were. The hole is a hole because we perceive it as a gap in what should be doughnut-space (let's call it 'dough-not'). In fact the hole is just air, but it is defined by what is around it: the context of doughnut makes it a 'dough-not'.

WHAT/EVER

Like most disciplines, philosophy has its own jargon. But sometimes philosophers also use ordinary words in ways that make them difficult to understand. So, instead of saying 'what exists, and why does "it" exist?' a philosopher might

> *say 'what exists and why does what exists exist?' This is*
> *more accurate, but harder to understand. What I have*
> *termed 'it' is really 'what exists now, or in the past, or in the*
> *future'. For convenience, and because in philosophy we're*
> *allowed to make things up, we'll call it 'what/ever'.*

Think about a poem that you have made up but not written down. It exists in your mind until you forget it or die. Does it have any form of existence (a) now and (b) when you have forgotten it or have died? What if you forgot it, but remembered it later? Would it have existed in between?

So it would seem that some things 'exist' as words or concepts (ideas) but not as physical phenomena.

As we can see, being sure of what exists is not quite as straightforward as it looks. Philosophers make it even harder by questioning the foundations of our judgements and beliefs and requiring proof that everything, even the enquiring mind, exists before accepting its claims.

Even when we believe in the existence of something, there is another question to ask – what can we know about it? We can see stars, but are they lights stuck on a celestial sphere as the ancients believed, or balls of gas undergoing nuclear fusion, as modern scientists tell us? How can we know what is true? This is the subject matter of epistemology, the study of knowledge (see Chapter 4).

A FALSE REALITY
In The Truman Show *(1998), a film directed by Peter Weir, an insurance salesman discovers that his entire life has been*

a TV show and nothing he supposed was real actually is real. In his thirtieth year, Truman begins to notice anomalies in his 'reality' and investigates them before attempting to escape his false world.

Dealing with it all

Once we've accepted that we exist, we have to deal with life. How should we live? Are there any universal moral laws that tell us how to behave? Or do different moral laws apply in different ages, places or circumstances? That is, is morality absolute or relative? Some things seem clear-cut. In most countries it's considered wrong to kill people. But some countries and certain states in the USA still have the death penalty and therefore endorse 'judicial killing'. Many people believe in a 'just war' – that we can go to war, inevitably causing some deaths, in support of a 'good' cause, such as deposing a tyrant. The victims of war or judicial execution don't generally want to die – and they are rarely given a choice. What about terminally ill people who ask to die? Is it right to kill them? Most countries don't allow this type of killing (euthanasia). How can it be defensible to wage a 'just war' in which a child playing in a marketplace is killed accidentally, but not defensible to kill an adult suffering chronic and incurable pain who wants to die? The questions of what is right and wrong, and how we make moral choices, is the subject matter of ethics (see Chapter 5).

The issue of how to live can be addressed on an individual and on a societal level. When it extends to issues about social cohesion and law, how a body of people should be governed, it becomes the material of political philosophy (see Chapter 6).

BRANCHES OF PHILOSOPHY

Metaphysics/ontology – the study of existence: what exists? What is it to exist?

Epistemology – the study of knowledge: what can we know and how do we know it?

Logic – the study of valid reasoning.

Ethics – the study of right and wrong actions: what should we do?

Politics – the study of force in society: what is allowed?

Aesthetics – the study of art/beauty.

Telling the story

Unlike other disciplines, philosophy does not always build on the ideas that have gone before. In physics, we could not have had Einstein without first having had Newton. In philosophy, anyone can start from scratch. The German philosopher Martin Heidegger, who published his one book in 1927, rejected everything that philosophers before him had said and set out to rebuild philosophy from the ground up. Someone else could do the same tomorrow. In one way this book doesn't offer any answers. Yet in another way it offers too many. It presents some of the answers that previous (and present) generations of philosophers have proposed, defended and sometimes overturned. In doing that, it provides a starting point for finding the answers which suit you – that can lead to 'the idea for which [you] can live and die'.

> 'I do not wish to judge how far my efforts coincide with those of other philosophers . . . the reason why I give no sources is that it is a matter of indifference to me whether the thoughts that I have had have been anticipated by someone else.'
>
> Ludwig Wittgenstein,
> *Tractatus Logico-Philosophicus* (1918)

CHAPTER 1
The problem of 'being'

—

'*Nothing exists except atoms and empty space; everything else is opinion.*'
Attributed to Democritus (*c*.460–370BC)

'*The question is: Why is there any being at all and not rather Nothing?*'
Martin Heidegger (1889–1976)

The nature of 'being' has concerned philosophers for at least 2,500 years and probably much longer. Although being and reality are close cousins, not all philosophers agree they are the same thing. Like so many terms in philosophy, they are open to discussion.

'Being', in the sense of existence, applies not just to humans but also to the physical world around us and the mental, emotional or spiritual world within us.

Reality might – or might not – be something that extends outside ourselves. How reality is constructed (that is, how our minds build a perception of reality) and how or whether it relates to anything real 'out there' are questions that get to the heart of being and 'what there is'. It remains possible that what we call 'reality' doesn't exist.

Is there anybody there?

The Ancient Greek philosopher Parmenides (c.510–c.440BC) was one of the first to tackle the question of what 'is', in a poem called 'On Nature'. In the poem, Parmenides describes reality as single, undivided, homogenous and unchanging. By way of a revelation delivered by a goddess, Parmenides says it is impossible to conceive of or describe something that doesn't exist because even thinking about it gives it some form of existence. This immediately leads us to question what we mean by 'being'.

Working from this idea – that just thinking of something means it 'is' – Parmenides presented the first known formal deduction in the history of Western philosophy. It goes like this:

- Thinking of something that 'is' implies the existence of something that 'is not' – if we say something 'is' a dog this implies that it 'is not' a cat.
- But we can't say something 'is not', as Parmenides has already demonstrated.

- Therefore, we can't say that something specific exists (because saying it 'is' something implies it 'is not' something else).
- Finally, as we can't discriminate between different things in the world, we can only see them as part of a continuous homogenous reality that has the property of existing. (You might think this is just a slick trick with words. If we didn't have words for 'cat' and 'dog', we wouldn't have the problem. But that's getting ahead of ourselves by more than 2,000 years.)

Similarly, things can't change. If we can think of something that will exist in the future, we are giving it some type of existence in our minds now. The same is true of the past: if you remember something that has gone, it exists in your memory. Indeed, everything that can be conceived of exists, even if only in the mind of one individual – and everything is part of one, unchanging, eternal whole.

Ideal Forms and the inferior world

Plato (c.427–347BC) adopted Parmenides' view that reality is unchanging and eternal. But he also recognized that we don't experience the world in that way, and that this disjunction between how the world is and how it seems must be explained.

Plato concluded that the world of experience is illusory. There is, he said, a realm of eternal, unchanging 'ideal Forms' which act as blueprints for everything that exists in the physical world. What we encounter with our senses are multiple individual instances or copies of the Forms. None of them is a perfect copy. According to Plato, although there are many individual horses, cats and dogs, they are all made in the image of the one universal Form of the 'horse', 'cat', or 'dog'. In a famous analogy, Plato likened the phenomena we experience to the shadows cast on the wall of a cave by firelight flickering behind objects. The ideal, or Form, is the equivalent of an object that casts a shadow; but we only ever see the shadow and never the object itself. We are not even aware that what we see is not 'reality'. This makes Plato an idealist – one who believes that 'reality' is what happens inside the mind or spirit: not the physical world around us, which is only created by our minds struggling to comprehend reality.

THE ALLEGORY OF THE CAVE

In his famous dialogue The Republic *(c.380BC), Plato describes a group of people who have spent their whole lives chained up inside a cave. All they can see are shadows cast on a wall by the light of a fire as people move around just out of view carrying objects such as carved figures of animals. The chained-up people come up with notions about the nature of reality, but all their ideas are based on the shadows they see and what they can infer from them. If one person were to free himself and see the world as it truly is, he would at first be blinded by the light and confused by what he saw, and find it hard to adapt. If he then returned to the cave, he would find it difficult to persuade the others that what they see is not reality. They would resist his lessons and even condemn him as mad. The person who escapes is, Plato said, like the philosopher who attempts to see beyond the shadows to the Forms – the true reality that lies behind what we see.*

As Plato extended the theory of Forms to everything, it follows that all individuals are made in the image of the universal Form of the human. This was easy for Christian thinkers to work with later, as it fits in with the Christian doctrine that all humans are made in the image of God. It helped one of the founders of the early Christian Church, St Augustine of Hippo (AD354–430), to accommodate Plato's metaphysics into a Christian schema and secure the Ancient Greek philosopher's enduring influence over European philosophy.

THERE'S NO SUCH THING AS MONSTERS . . .

Suppose you create a monster in your mind. You know the monster does not 'really' exist – it has no external, physical existence in the world – as you've just made it up. But in imagining the monster, you give it some form of existence. Clearly existence in the world, in the mind and in language are very different.

We can say a cat exists because cats are familiar to us in the real world. We can say a unicorn exists as they are depicted in literature and art, with established qualities and physical appearance. The monster you have thought up, un-named, undrawn, unarticulated – does it have any form of existence? If so, what? This question still occupies philosophers in the present day.

Early audiences of F. W. Murnau's silent film Nosferatu *(1922) felt real fear, even though they knew the vampire didn't exist.*

Plato didn't restrict his theory to physical objects. He also thought there were ideal Forms of concepts such as beauty, justice and truth, and even of mathematical ideas such as number and class. As recently as the 20th century, Gottlob Frege (1848–1925) and Kurt Gödel (1906–78) endorsed this aspect of Plato's thoughts, considering numbers to have absolute reality as Forms.

Plato maintained that there was a separate realm, apart from the observable physical universe, where these Forms lurked. Where might that be? One possibility is that they might be outside time and space. Later, neoplatonists, such as Plotinus and St Augustine, claimed that these Forms reside in the mind of God.

NEOPLATONISM

Neoplatonism is a philosophy that follows the work of Plato but extends or adapts it, focusing on spiritual and mystical aspects. It is generally considered to have started with the work of Plotinus (c.AD204–270).

THE PROBLEM OF UNIVERSALS – OR 'IS THERE SUCH A THING AS RED?'
The English friar and philosopher William of Ockham, who died in 1347, took a view that was directly opposite to that of Plato. He stated that universals do not exist outside human understanding, and that terms such as 'redness', or even 'man' are just ways of collecting together many individual objects for psychological simplicity. In reality there are only individuals, and all types of categorization are imposed and artificial.

In modern terminology, this makes Ockham a nominalist – someone for whom the only existence of universals is as a name for something. Plato, on the other hand, was a realist – someone who believes universals have existence.

WHAT'S IN A NAME?
Nominalism states that non-physical concepts such as 'justice', 'green' or 'twelve' have no existence beyond the words that name them. It's possible to have a severe case of nominalism, or only slight nominalism.

Predicate nominalists say that green things are green only because the predicate green is applied to all of them. (A predicate *is a word describing a property of a subject.) 'Green' has no existence outside the word, and there is nothing other than the use of the word that unites green things. This leaves unanswered how we decide to apply the word 'green' to something, but allows that two people might not experience the same thing when they look at something 'green'.*

Resemblance nominalists say that things are called 'green' if they sufficiently resemble an exemplar (Plato's ideal Form) of 'green', and if they resemble that more than they resemble another, competing, exemplar, such as 'purple'.

The Ancient Greek philosopher Aristotle was also a realist, but of a different flavour. Aristotle believed that universals only had existence if they were 'instantiated' (that is, if there were real, tangible instances of them), whereas Plato believed universals have absolute existence, independently of their instantiation. Suppose all human life were extinguished. For Plato, universals such as childhood, cruelty and chastity would still exist, but for Aristotle they would not exist, as they could not be instantiated – there would no longer be real, tangible examples to draw on.

All, nothing or something?

Plato's pupil Aristotle picked the common-sense position that is the default for most people in their everyday dealings with the world. He argued that reality exists independently of the human mind, and makes up the world of physical objects and phenomena that we find around us. For Aristotle, matter exists and it is given 'substantial form' by some kind of organizing principle. It is this organizing principle that gives different types of matter their distinctive properties and 'potentialities' or powers. Therefore, the physical material that makes up everything, from tables to giraffes, is the same, while the 'substantial form' gives some things 'table-ness' and other things 'giraffe-ness'.

To summarize, there are two opposing positions in relation to reality:

Idealism (Plato): Everything we experience in the world and think of as reality is an illusion created by our imperfect senses; the realm of ideal Forms is not directly accessible to us.
Realism (Aristotle): The external world exists independently of humans being present to experience it. Universals exist only when they are instantiated – so if all red things were to vanish, red itself would no longer exist.

These two basic positions have given rise to different variants and emphases since the time of the Ancient Greeks. Between the polar extremes of idealism and realism, there is a dualist position that allows both matter and something insubstantial to exist. In fact, dualism is more than one position – there are plenty of variants. But in essence it sees a distinction between the physical and the non-physical (particularly but not exclusively in terms of the human), then struggles to build bridges between them. The question that most troubles dualists is, how can the physical interact with the non-physical, and vice versa? Yet everyday common sense tells us that it does. If you fall down and break a leg, it causes physical damage and pain. It also makes you miserable, frustrated, angry –

mental states apparently caused by a physical state or event. Dualism is covered in more detail in Chapter 3.

MULTIPLE REALITIES

The American philosopher David Kellogg-Lewis (1941–2001) went beyond the concept of 'all or nothing' and opted for an 'even more than all' position. Adapting the 'many worlds' theory proposed by physicist Hugh Everett, he claimed that all possible worlds exist and are real, though spatially and temporally separate. He believed that all these worlds have equivalent concrete reality. Kellogg considered that an innate understanding of this state of affairs is evident in us ever considering statements such as the following to be true: 'If I had eaten that very old sandwich, I would have been sick.' In philosophical terms, this statement is a 'counterfactual conditional'. The statement supposes that there is another world in which 'I' did eat the sandwich and was sick.

In the 'many worlds' theory, there are worlds in which Germany won World War II, in which the dinosaurs were not wiped out, and worlds in which you were never born.

What do we mean by 'existence'?

With Aristotle, philosophers stopped looking at 'being' *per se*, and began to consider how we can *know* what exists. Then, in 1927, the German philosopher Martin Heidegger (1889–1976) suggested that Western philosophy had been concentrating on the wrong kind of questions since the age of Plato. While Plato's metaphysics and Aristotle's epistemology had centred on what exists, what we can know about what exists, and what properties those 'things' have, Heidegger said we need to take a step back and to ask first what we mean by 'existence' or 'being'. As he focused on the question 'What is being?' he realized that we also have to ask why there is something rather than nothing. If we were designing philosophy from the ground up, these would be the first questions to ask. So Heidegger decided to overturn the philosophical legacy of the preceding 2,500 years and start afresh.

Aristotle had talked of 'being as such', meaning the essence of being without regard to any specific type of being (neither the 'being' that is living – a person or a dog, say – nor the being that is inanimate existence – a table or a pen). Heidegger would start from there.

THE BEING IN THE WORLD

Heidegger used the term *Dasein* – a German word that means 'being there' – for the being that exists. He rejected the idea that there is an external world separate from a conscious observer (the position of Cartesian dualism). Instead, he developed a phenomenological view, in which our understanding of things is always in relation to ourselves. For example, if you put on a jumper, it is because the jumper will keep you warm, or you think it will look good on you. It is not because the jumper is made of twisted yarn and a few millimetres thick – that is of no interest or relevance to you. This theory applies to knowledge, too. We might read a book about politics because it interests us, or because understanding politics helps us make sense of what we see happening around us. We see it in terms of a tool, or satisfying a need.

Heidegger saw the *Dasein* (principally the human 'being') as completely immersed in and part of the world that defines it. No separation between consciousness and environment is possible. 'Being *there*' means that 'there' – our context – is the defining aspect of 'being'. We are not shut off from the world in an enclosed mind, which Heidegger calls the 'cabinet of consciousness'. For him, the distinction between 'out there' (in the world) and 'inside' (in our minds) was invalid.

There is, however, a difference between the 'being' of an animate creature and an inanimate object. A chair or a ship has static being, but humans are aware of passing, finite time; a moment in time is part of the 'there' we inhabit. Our consciousness of our own being is defined by time and by the knowledge that we will die. This aspect of Heidegger's thinking was taken up by existentialists such as Jean-Paul Sartre (1905–80) and Albert Camus (1913–60).

Martin Heidegger is considered one of the greatest philosophers of the 20th century.

'The perception of what is known does not take place as a return with one's booty to the "cabinet" of consciousness after one has gone out and grasped it. Rather, in perceiving, preserving and retaining, the Da-sein that knows remains outside as Da-sein. In "mere" knowledge about a context of the being of beings . . . in "solely" thinking about it, I am no less outside in the world together with beings than I am when I originally grasp them. Even forgetting something, when every relation of being to what was previously

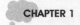

> *known seems to be extinguished, must be understood as a modification of primordial being-in, and this holds true for every deception and every error.'*
>
> Martin Heidegger, *Being and Time* (1927)

Why is there?

Once we have asked 'what is there?' then, unless the answer is 'nothing', we are bound to ask 'why is there?' (whatever 'there' is), and 'why am I?'

We can't know when humans first started to ask questions such as 'why do I exist?' or 'what makes me alive?' It was probably long before written culture began. The earliest answers to those questions that we know of are religious. Perhaps once people began to make things from clay or wood or bone, the inevitable next step was to posit a superhuman entity to try to explain how they themselves came to be 'made'. An individual who feels the wonder of existence, who is aware of inspiration, love, hate, hope and despair – and who believes there is a spirit animating himself or herself – might well come to believe that this spirit is somehow the cause and purpose of existence.

FIRST MISTAKES

The Greek philosopher Andronicus of Rhodes collected Aristotle's works around 60BC. It's thought he put the writings on 'first philosophy' straight after Aristotle's Physics, and therefore called them τὰ μετὰ τὰ φυσικὰ βιβλία (ta meta ta physika biblia) or 'the books that come after the [books on] physics' This was later confusingly shortened to 'meta physika' or 'beyond physics', giving us the term 'metaphysics'.

First movers

The origin and cause of all things is often called the 'first mover' or 'prime mover'. For the religious, the first mover is a god. That can put a stop to further questions in a religion that doesn't allow its believers to question the origins or purposes of their god. The Greeks had legends to explain the existence of their gods, but still had to come back to a first mover. In some versions, the job was given to Chronos (time), and Chaos (the void), with the primeval gods coming from one or both of these entities. The idea that the universe formed out of time and space or chaos is remarkably close to modern cosmological theory.

A 'WHY' WITHOUT GODS

The first person known to have looked for a non-mystical explanation for the existence of things is the philosopher Thales (c.624–c.546BC), who was born in the Ancient Greek port of Miletus (now in Turkey). He is considered the father of Western philosophy. If Thales wrote anything, none of it survives: we know of his life and ideas only through reports made by Aristotle and other Ancient Greek writers such as the historians Herodotus (484–425BC) and Plutarch (c.AD46–120), and particularly the 3rd-century BC biographer Diogenes Laertius. But it seems from them that Thales' approach was ground-breaking. In an age when society explained the nature of the world through stories about the wills and whims of anthropomorphic gods, Thales sought to find a common, underlying principle to explain the world around him.

Aristotle reports that Thales thought the Earth floated on water, just as a log or a ship floats on the sea. So instead of earthquakes being caused by angry gods, Thales proposed that the land was rocked by waves from underneath – a view remarkably close in some ways to modern plate tectonics in which earthquakes are explained by the movement of the Earth's plates on a bed of fluid magma. Well, he was wrong about the water, but the principle – that the physical processes of the world can be ascribed to natural, not supernatural, causes – laid the foundations of modern science.

BEAN COUNTER

Thales died around 546BC, by which time the Ancient Greek philosopher and mathematician Pythagoras (*c.*570–495BC) was around 25 years old. He, too, sought an explicable basis for the natural world and found it in numbers, much as modern-day scientists attempt to explain the forces of the universe in terms of mathematical rules. Pythagoras mingled his maths with a fair dose of mysticism, and the school he founded was distinctly cultish. His followers were not allowed to touch a white cockerel, look into a mirror set beside a light, or eat beans (see panel below).

Pythagoras had a strong belief in the transmigration of souls – the idea that the soul survived death and entered another living creature, which might be human or animal. Vegetarianism was the inevitable outcome of this belief, as any potential meaty meal could house the soul of a former (or future) friend or relative.

THE SACRED BEAN
Pythagoras held beans to be sacred. He banned the eating of meat and of beans by his followers. Several reasons for this have been suggested, including that 'they are like genitals' (testicles) or that 'they are like the gates of Hades, [the stems] alone [of all plants] being without joints' (both from Aristotle). This last point possibly meant that the hollow stem of a bean plant was considered the conduit

for souls on their way to being transmigrated. This would explain Pythagoras' injunction to protect both beans and bean plants from animals, and the legend that he allowed his enemies to kill him rather than run away through a bean field, which would have damaged the beans.

METAPHYSICS AND PHYSICS

Thales and Pythagoras set humankind on the path to what we now call science (from the Latin *'scienta'*, meaning 'knowledge'). The scientific way of thinking is a branch of philosophy. Indeed, until the late 19th century, scientific endeavour was called 'natural philosophy'. The subject of natural philosophy emerged alongside scientific thinking: something that aims to discover what is demonstrably true. The first professorial chair in Natural Philosophy was at the University of Padua, in 1577. When Pythagoras concluded that the universe ran according to laws that are independent of human knowledge of them, he did not have the resources to prove it – it was a theory and a belief, much as the existence of the Greek gods was a theory and a belief. When Newton concluded the same thing, he was able to use mathematics and scientific instruments to demonstrate that these rules do appear to exist. The movements of the planets follow certain rules. The movement of a falling body, or a cannonball shot from a cannon, also follows rules.

METAPHYSICS

Metaphysics means 'beyond the physical world'. This branch of philosophy deals with questions of being, reality and existence. It is what Aristotle called 'first philosophy'.

NOT QUITE THERE

Science has a non-mystical explanation for how the universe and life on Earth came about. But that still doesn't answer the basic questions: Where did the 'what/ever' of the Big Bang come from? Why did it come about? How and why did life emerge from inanimate chemicals?

Whether we personally prefer the religious or scientific explanation for the origins of life and the universe, both stumble over the question: where did the 'first mover' (God/material of the Big Bang) come from? And why? Religion says 'don't ask, it's a mystery, it's beyond understanding'; science says 'we don't know yet'. Both sometimes say 'it was always there' or that 'time and space/God have no start and no end'. For this reason, religion and science are not necessarily mutually exclusive.

Does God exist?

—

*'If I saw no signs of a divinity, I would fix
myself in denial. If I saw everywhere the marks
of a Creator, I would repose peacefully in faith. But seeing
too much to deny Him, and too little to assure me, I am in a
pitiful state, and I would wish a hundred times that if a God
sustains nature it would reveal Him without ambiguity.'*
Blaise Pascal, *Pensées* (1669)

CHAPTER 2

'The interest I have to believe a thing is no proof that such a thing exists.'
Voltaire, *Remarks on the Thoughts of Pascal* XI

One answer often given to the question 'why is there?' is 'God.' It also applies to *what* is there?' – does the what there is include a God? And if so, what is that God like?

There are several approaches to God and to whether or not He exists:

- The complexity of the world or the universe and all that is in it indicates a designer, since it is inconceivable that such a system would come about by chance (the cosmological argument).
- Everything has to be caused by something, so there must be a first cause, and that is what we shall call God (the teleological argument).
- Because we can imagine a God, there must be one (the ontological argument).
- Faith – inner personal conviction tells us there is a God so there must be.

None of these 'proofs' is satisfactory in philosophical terms, and there are several problems with the notion of 'God' that philosophers have attempted to answer – again, not entirely satisfactorily.

For those who believe in God, the paucity of the arguments for God's existence is no reason for giving up on Him. Indeed, the very nature of faith is that it stands outside reason, so if God does exist, His existence need not be susceptible to proof.

THEISM

Theism is the belief in a single god who is omnipotent (all powerful), omniscient (all knowing) and benevolent. Christianity, Judaism and Islam are all theistic religions.

I think, therefore He is

For many philosophers throughout history, belief in God was the default position – they lived in societies in which the existence of God was not generally doubted, and in some cases even to question it was a crime. St Anselm (1033–1109), who was archbishop of Canterbury from 1093, was the first to try to prove the existence of God by reason.

By Anselm's time, the works of Plato and Aristotle had been rediscovered and the Christian philosophers, called scholastics, were attempting to integrate them into their theology.

It is said that after studying the Greek philosophers, Anselm's students wanted to hear a rational justification for the existence of God. Aristotle and Plato had cited the complexity of the world as evidence of the existence of their gods. Anselm's reply – the ontological argument for the existence of God – has become one of the most debated issues in philosophy.

Suppose that by the term 'God' we mean the greatest, most powerful thing we can think of. The existence of God would then seem to follow necessarily from the definition because:

- A God imagined that does not exist is not as great as one imagined that does exist.
- It would be a contradiction to suppose that God is both the greatest thing that can be thought of and also does not exist.

- Since we can clearly think of God and suppose He
  exists, then He must exist.

There's obviously something wrong with this argument. Anselm's first critic was a contemporary, the Benedictine monk Gaunilo of Marmoutiers. He argued that if Anselm's reasoning were correct, we could imagine a lost island that was the most perfect island there could ever be. Since by definition it is the most perfect, it must exist as otherwise it would be less than perfect. As Anselm's reasoning could lead to the existence of all sorts of imaginary objects, it must be at fault. In response, Anselm said that perfection only applies to God, so the ontological argument can't be used to prove the existence of imaginary islands or anything other than God.

SCHOLASTICISM

The scholastics were Christian philosophers working in the medieval universities (c.1100–1500). Their method, scholasticism, proceeds through the dialectic approach – asking a question, proposing an answer, refuting that answer, and so on, to arrive at a conclusion. The scholastics' aim was to bring together two broad sources of authority: Christian (the Bible and the writings of the Church Fathers) and classical (principally Aristotle and Plato, the latter filtered through the neoplatonists).

ONTOLOGY

Ontology is the study of existence and of what exists.

> 'Nor do I seek to understand that I may believe, but I believe that I may understand. For this, too, I believe, that, unless I first believe, I shall not understand.'
>
> St Anselm of Canterbury,
> *Discourse (Proslogion)* (1077–8)

ONGOING DEBATE

Many philosophers agree that the problem with Anselm's argument concerns making the meaning of a word or concept the basis on which we decide whether something exists, an objection raised by Thomas Aquinas (1225–74). But philosophers and logicians still debate exactly which logical error is involved. For philosophy, the obvious fact that something is nonsensical isn't good enough – it must be possible to prove that it's nonsense if it is to be dismissed.

The French philosopher and mathematician René Descartes (1596–1650) is often called the father of modern philosophy. He had his own version of the ontological argument that was extremely simple – so simple, in fact, that it is more a self-evident axiom. He says that because the essence of a supreme being includes that it exists, then God must exist. The argument is built on other assertions, including one which states that the idea of God is native to the mind.

The German philosopher Immanuel Kant (1724–1804) pointed out that as essence does not presuppose existence, the essence of a supreme being can be what it likes – it doesn't mean the supreme being has to exist. In addition, the argument presupposes that existence is an attribute of perfection – perhaps it is not. Even so, the ontological argument has sufficient appeal that philosophers keep returning to it.

In the 1960s, the American philosopher Norman Malcolm (1911–90) revived a variant of the argument which avoids previous objections. He redefined God as an 'absolutely unlimited being' and then proceeded as follows:

- Any being whose existence depended on something else or who could be prevented from existing by something else, would be limited and therefore could not be God.
- For any proposed being, existence can be possible (but not necessary), necessary, or impossible.
- If its existence is possible but not necessary, the being exists in some possible worlds but not in others. Its non-existence in the others suggests something, or the lack of something, prevents it from existing, so it is not an unlimited being.
- If something that is 'possible but not necessary' is not an unlimited being, God's existence can't be 'possible but not necessary'.
- God is therefore either impossible or necessarily exists.

The task remains to prove that God is not impossible.

Ground zero

Another critic of Anselm's ontological argument was St Thomas Aquinas, who was uncomfortable with its requirement that mere humans have to be able to conceive of God, who is transcendent and therefore inconceivable. Aquinas' criticism of the ontological argument was so thorough that Anselm's position completely lost credibility for several centuries, resurfacing with Descartes, only to be rebuffed again.

Aquinas presented perhaps the most lucid and concise logical arguments for the existence of God. His 'Five Ways', or five

Immanuel Kant maintained that what a thing is essentially 'like' is not connected to whether it exists.

steps, to proving God exists appear in his *Summa Theologica*. He did not consider these absolute proofs, but steps on the way towards a proof. He developed the cosmological argument from Aristotle's contention that there must be a 'first mover' which put everything else in motion.

The first way proves the existence of God through the existence of change:

- Some things in the world are in the process of change.
- Change must be caused by something else, as a thing can't spontaneously change of its own accord.
- This cause must itself be initiated by something.
- We must continue this chain of cause and effect *ad infinitum* unless we posit a 'first mover'. That first mover is God.

The second way is similar to the first. It assumes that a thing can't cause itself, but must have an external cause. It ends, rather paradoxically, by concluding there must be one thing which causes itself and that thing is God. Several philosophers have complained that Aquinas' thinking is confused as the proposition he seeks to prove is the very proposition he denies in the course of the argument.

> *'If the hand does not move the stick, the stick will not move anything else.'*
> Thomas Aquinas, *Summa Theologica* (1266–73)

The third way relies on change:

- We notice in the world that things come into being and also cease to exist.
- Clearly, not everything can be transient or there would have been a time when nothing existed, and nothing could be generated from that – something cannot come from nothing.
- Something must always have existed, and that something is what we call God.

This recalls the argument made by the Ancient Greek philosopher Parmenides that nothing can come out of nothing, so something (being) must have always existed. These first three ways are variations of the cosmological argument.

The fourth way is a version of Anselm's ontological argument:

- Things can exhibit varying degrees of a quality, such as being more or less hot or good.
- Varying degrees of a quality are caused by something that itself exhibits the perfect amount of a quality – so the Sun, which is the hottest thing, bestows heat on other things.

- For some things to exhibit goodness, there must be a thing that is entirely 'good' and that thing is God.

The fifth way draws on Aristotle's notion of *telos*, or purpose, and is a teleological argument:

- All things aim towards some ultimate goal or end.
- Some mind must direct or intend that purpose; it is God that lies behind it.

TELEOLOGICAL ARGUMENT
A teleological argument is one that relates to purpose, intention or aims.

Thomas Aquinas (1225–74)
Thomas Aquinas was born in Sicily, educated at the universities of Naples and Cologne, and went on to lecture at Paris and Naples. He was canonized in 1323 by Pope John XII.

*   Much of Aquinas' work is derived from Aristotle and consists of trying to reconcile Aristotle's thinking with Christian teaching (a reconciliation that Augustine achieved for Plato's works). Aquinas also clarified and extended Aristotle's ideas. His huge* Summa Theologica, *or* Summary of Theology, *contains the 'Five Ways', perhaps the clearest attempt ever to prove the existence of God through logical argument. The first part of the* Summa *discusses God, creation and human nature; the second part*

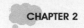

> *deals with morality; and the third part begins to deal with*
> *Christ and the sacraments. Aquinas never finished the third*
> *part, giving up one day after experiencing a mystical vision*
> *compared to which, he said, all he had written seemed*
> *like straw.*

Although modern philosophers have almost all rejected Aquinas' Five Ways, the Catholic Church still holds to versions of them.

By the end of the 13th century, then, cosmological, teleological and ontological arguments for the existence of God had been put forward. What came after were largely refinements of these arguments, attempts to bolster them or critical assaults on them. A few other claims – such as that miracles prove divinity – don't really constitute arguments for the existence of God. (If we accept that a miracle has occurred, it only demonstrates the veracity of miracles, not of God.)

NOT THE FIRST . . .

Aquinas was not the first post-classical proponent of the
first-cause theory. The Muslim philosopher Avicenna, or
Ibn Sīnā (c.AD980–1037), attempted to integrate elements
of Aristotle's and Plato's philosophy with his religious belief
in God as the Creator. The commentaries of Avicenna and
contemporary Muslim scholars were translated into Latin
and entered Europe through Spain, greatly influencing the
work of Aquinas and the scholastics. Avicenna's argument
to prove the existence of God is remarkably similar to that
of Aquinas:

- *Things come in and out of existence, so existence is not itself an essential property.*
- *If something comes into existence, there must be a cause for it happening.*
- *There can't be an infinite chain of caused events without a first cause setting them off.*
- *This first cause is self-existent and is, of course, God.*

DAMNED IF YOU DON'T – PASCAL'S WAGER

Whether or not God exists is not a purely philosophical question. For anyone who believes in a God who takes an interest in humans and doles out rewards and punishments, the existence or non-existence of God is usually tied up with the possibility of an afterlife, and hence of eternal damnation or salvation. This conviction focuses the mind more effectively than simple intellectual curiosity.

The French rationalist Blaise Pascal (1623–62) generally supported a rigorously scientific approach to knowledge, but held that different rules apply when we talk about God. In matters beyond the reach of reason, Pascal said that all we can do is rely on the authority of sacred texts. In fact, he was a deeply religious man and in the last years of his life spent much of his time putting together his *Thoughts* (*Pensées*). These make up a collection of jottings rather than a single, narrative argument, and are a form of *apologia* for Christianity. In them he deals with the limitations of reason and the lack of absolute certainty.

APOLOGIA

An apologia, *or* apology, *is a reasoned argument in defence of a position.*

The most influential point in *Pensées* is Pascal's 'wager' about the existence of God. It is not an argument for the existence of God so much as a recommendation for belief in God as a rational position. Either God exists or He does not. We can't discover which is true from reason, but we must choose either to believe or not believe. We must make a wager:

- If God does not exist, we lose nothing by believing that He does – death brings annihilation whether we believe in God or not.
- But if He does exist, then we stand to gain everything (salvation) by believing that He does, and to lose everything (damnation) by thinking that He doesn't.
- It is therefore sensible to act as though God does exist: 'If you gain, you gain all; if you lose, you lose nothing.'

'I should be much more afraid of being mistaken and then finding out that Christianity is true than of being mistaken in believing it to be true.'

Blaise Pascal, *Pensées* (1669)

One obvious objection to Pascal's wager, made around a hundred years later by the French philosopher Denis Diderot (1713–84), is that there are many wagers to be made. Pascal dealt only with the God of Catholic Christianity, but there are and have been many different gods and belief systems throughout history and we need to choose one of them. Pascal might make his wager and live according to the dictates of the Catholic Church, but he might then die and be damned because he should have been following Krishna or Thor or Zeus.

CHOOSING THE BETTER WAY

The American psychologist and philosopher William James (1842–1910), brother of the novelist Henry James, proposed another pragmatic approach to belief. He saw life as full of choices, some of which were 'forced', by which he meant that an answer must be given as sitting on the fence is not an option. He saw belief in God as a forced choice – if you don't choose to believe you have chosen the other option, non-belief.

Some choices were also 'momentous' – they made a huge difference to life. The decision to believe in God was one he regarded as momentous, arguing that choosing to believe gave a person a moral and psychological structure, enriched their life and gave them purpose. He saw nothing to be gained by non-belief, so the sensible person would always choose to believe. James' reasoning is even shakier than Pascal's, as it does not promote one religion over another, nor does it promote religion of any kind over another scheme that might give a person's life focus and purpose.

No need of proof

For some philosophers, the whole concept of proving the existence of God has been either anathema or irrelevant. One such was the Dutch Christian humanist Desiderius Erasmus (1466–1536). Erasmus was particularly impatient with the hypocrisy and worldliness of the Catholic Church, and had no truck with the scholastics and their dealings with Plato and Aristotle. Rather, he aligned himself with Augustine and his simple avowals of faith.

For Erasmus, belief in God was not a matter of reason but of pure faith. His book *In Praise of Folly* (1509) satirizes and criticizes the Church, attacking the monastic orders for their apparent belief that living a good religious life consisted of 'the precise number of knots to the tying on their sandals'. Instead, he argues, true religion is 'worship from the heart' and does not need the Church as intermediary. Religion is a form of folly in that it is simple, direct and not snarled up in complex doctrine. It must be based on pure, thorough humanism – confidence in the power of the human spirit to recognize and worship God.

> 'It will be pretty to hear their pleas before the great tribunal: one will brag how he mortified his carnal appetite by feeding only upon fish: another will urge that he spent most of his time on earth in the divine exercise of singing psalms . . . but Christ will interrupt: "Woe unto you, scribes and Pharisees, I left you but one precept, of loving one another, which I do not hear anyone plead that he has faithfully discharged."'
>
> Desiderius Erasmus, *In Praise of Folly* (1509)

Erasmus was as much concerned with the institution of the Church as with proving the existence of God, but the idea that the spirit naturally comprehends and yearns towards God became a powerful non-rational argument for God's existence.

HOW MANY ANGELS CAN DANCE ON THE POINT OF A NEEDLE?

It's difficult to exaggerate the levels of intricacy and ingenuity in scholastic and theological arguments. However, the suggestion that philosophers debated how many angels could dance on the point of a needle or the head of a pin does not seem to be borne out by the surviving texts. The earliest reference to this supposed question is in the mid-17th century:

'And Schibler, with others, maketh the difference of extension to be this, that Angels can contract their whole substance into one part of space, and therefore have not partes extra partes. Whereupon it is that the Schoolmen have questioned how many Angels may fit upon the point of a Needle?'

Richard Baxter, *The Reasons of the Christian Religion*
(1667)

It's possible that the question was an exercise used to train young scholars in the art of debate, or that it existed only in parodic form to mock the nicety or absurdity of the questions being debated.

Faith and reason

While Erasmus objected to the Church's way of dealing with religion, he was not denying the central beliefs of Christianity – the literal existence of God, the physical incarnation of Christ, and so on. A move away from the precise formulation of the divine presented by religious doctrine and authority marked the Age of Enlightenment, which began soon after Erasmus' death.

The French philosopher François-Marie Arouet (1694–1778), better known by his pen name 'Voltaire', was among those to take a more liberal view of God. He did not feel that belief in any particular brand of religion was necessary for an understanding of the divine. Neither, interestingly, did he think that blind faith was necessary. He was able to reconcile his belief in the divine with his trust that everything in both the physical and moral/spiritual spheres is governed by explicable if not yet discovered laws:

'What is faith? Is it to believe that which is evident? No. It is perfectly evident to my mind that there exists a necessary, eternal, supreme and intelligent being. This is no matter of faith, but of reason.'

The Jewish-Dutch philosopher Baruch Spinoza (1632–77) was also keen to affirm the existence of a divinity (and was a fan of the ontological argument for that purpose) but disinclined to follow any particular body of religious teaching. He is often considered to be the original pantheist, though this simplifies his position somewhat. Spinoza believed that all there is forms one whole, and that the whole is a supreme divine being. This means that while the natural world is God, it is not all God is – rather, it's a subset of God. The opposite of Judeo-Christian belief, Spinoza's God had no anthropomorphic qualities – no personality, no incarnation, no will nor intentions, no consciousness. Everything that happens follows necessarily from the nature, rather than the will of God, following immutable laws not of his making. To all intents and purposes, this made Spinoza an

Most medieval scholars linked science, in particular astronomy, astrology and geometry, to the divine.

atheist in 17th-century terms and in 1656 he was expelled from the Jewish community by *cherem* (excommunication and curse) for his 'monstrous deeds' and 'abominable heresies'.

> **PANTHEISM**
> *Pantheism is the belief that God is manifest in the whole of the natural universe and inseparable from it. God is not anthropomorphized and has no will, purpose or consciousness.*

While Voltaire found belief in God to be an act of reason, Søren Kierkegaard (1813–55) held religion to be a matter of passion. Reason can only undermine faith, he claimed, and can never justify it. Rationalistic proofs of God's existence, such as those given by Anselm or Aquinas, have nothing at all to do with a belief in God. An authentic belief acquires its force from within, as a 'leap of faith', without reason reassuring us that what we are doing is the right thing. If God's existence were susceptible to rational reflection, there would be no need for faith and it would be meaningless.

Despite this fiercely religious spirit, Kierkegaard attacked the organized Church, which he considered to be the very antithesis of Christianity. He felt that the trappings – attending church, reciting scripture and so on – have nothing to do with the religious life, which must involve a personal and direct confrontation with the divine.

God is dead – or was never there

Of course, one reason it might be difficult to prove the existence of God is that He doesn't exist. This is a position that has been difficult for philosophers to take in many times and places. In a thoroughly en-godded society (that is, one in which belief in God is universal), a philosopher who stands up to say 'there is no God' might at best be ridiculed and at worst executed. But that option became available around the 18th century, once the Age of Enlightenment was well underway and the stranglehold of the Church had begun to loosen. In some circles it even became rather fashionable to deny the existence of God.

THE AGE OF ENLIGHTENMENT
The Age of Enlightenment is the name given to a period, starting around 1650, marked by growing confidence in the power of human reason and the possibilities offered by new scientific discoveries and ways of thinking. Also known as the Age of Reason, it saw scepticism, science and intellectual rigour replace superstition, faith and a blind acceptance of classical authority. Thinkers considered instrumental in triggering the Age of Enlightenment are Spinoza, Voltaire, Newton and Locke. It had its beginnings principally in France and England, and spread from there to other European centres and to North America.

The Scottish philosopher David Hume (1711–76) was one of the first to deny the existence of God openly. Hume was an arch-sceptic and rejected anything that could not be gathered from personal sensory experience. This meant throwing the baby Jesus out with the bathwater. The bathwater was a slop that included the existence of the self, logical necessity, causation and the validity of inductive knowledge itself. In Hume's *Dialogues Concerning Natural Religion* (1779), the sceptical character Philo puts forward objections to all the main arguments that are said to demonstrate the existence of God. Hume was slightly too early with his provocative stance, which is why the work was first published three years after his death.

By the time the German philosopher Friedrich Nietzsche (1844–1900) was writing, denial of God's existence might have been unpopular but was no longer as dangerous as it had been for Spinoza. Nietzsche's father, a Protestant minister, died when his son was just four, and the boy was brought up in austere Lutheran piety by his mother and sister. He became especially hostile towards Christianity, which he labelled a 'slave morality'. By this he meant that it had grown out of the bitterness and resentment of the oppressed and weak. Instead of addressing their low status in society or having the inner strength to master their resentment, the oppressed had invented a scheme in which their oppressors would be punished in some imagined future life. According to Nietzsche, in a slave morality the oppressed denigrate the qualities or characteristics that give others power over them and elevate the opposite characteristics. Therefore wealth and power are bad, and poverty and humility are good. Those who demonstrate the bad attributes will be punished after death, and those who demonstrate the good attributes will be rewarded.

Nietzsche is not the only one to have seen religion as a distraction to keep the masses quiet. The German political philosopher Karl Marx's famous remark that religion is 'the opium of the people' carries the same sentiment, except that instead of religion emerging from the oppressed consciousness, Marx has it being force-fed to the proletariat by the establishment.

Marx followed the claim made by philosopher and anthropologist Ludwig Feuerbach (1804–72) that human beings had created God in their own image and that worshipping God diverted them from enjoying their own human powers. He criticized Feuerbach, though, for failing to understand why people are lured into following religions. According to Marx, it is a sense of alienation in material life that drives people to seek solace in spiritual life. He saw this alienation occurring in two ways: alienation of labour and social alienation. The second of these is the failure of contemporary society to acknowledge and exercise the innate communal nature of people. Human beings exist as a community, and life is only possible because we rely on a vast network of social and economic relations. Marx sees the need for community 'deviously acknowledged' by religion, which creates a false idea of a community in which we are all equal in the eyes of God.

> 'Religion is the sigh of the oppressed creature, the heart of a heartless world, and the soul of soulless conditions. It is the opium of the people.'
>
> Karl Marx, *German–French Annals*,
> written with Arnold Ruge (1844)

The civic state offers another illusion of community in which we are all equal in the eyes of the law. When people are truly emancipated and can realize a true form of community, religion will naturally wither away. The Russian anarchist revolutionary Mikhail Bakunin (1814–76) was even more anti-God than Marx, seeing him as the (imaginary) incarnation of pretty much all the ills ever visited upon humankind.

> 'The idea of God implies the abdication of human reason and justice; it is the most decisive negation of human liberty, and necessarily ends in the enslavement of mankind, in theory and practice.'
>
> Mikhail Bakunin, *God and the State* (1882)

Mikhail Bakunin was a Russian revolutionary philosopher, considered by many to be the originator of anarchist theory. Anarchism holds the state to be undesirable in all its forms.

BECAUSE GOD DIDN'T EXIST, WE CREATED HIM

The Austrian psychologist Sigmund Freud (1856–1939) also believed God to be an invention of the human mind, but arising through personal need rather than political manipulation. He described religion as a necessary illusion that helps to restrain our sexual and destructive tendencies. It derives, he argued, from our longing for a father figure to 'exorcize the terrors of nature . . . reconcile men to the cruelty of Fate . . . and compensate them for the sufferings [of] civilized life.'

NON-REALIST RATHER THAN NON-REAL

Another option, proposed by the German philosopher Georg Hegel (1770–1831), is to redefine God. Called the non-realist view of God, Hegel's view states that God is not something that exists independently but is a way of talking about a set of moral or spiritual ideas. This view has been criticized as disguised atheism, and certainly requires a major overhaul of our definition of God and what religion offers. If God doesn't exist in any kind of separate 'out there' sense, then nor does heaven or hell, and the existence or otherwise of miracles has no connection with religion. It is a view that has found favour with a number of modern thinkers, even including some members of the clergy.

'To speak of God is to speak about the moral and spiritual goals we ought to be aiming at, and about what we ought to become. . . . The true God is not God as picturesque supernatural fact, but God as our religious ideal.'

Don Cupitt, *The Sea of Faith* (1988)

Pick a god, any god

If we accept any of the arguments for the existence of God, we have a starting point for religion. But none of the evidence offered by the philosophers proves the existence of the very precise God each of them would like to promote. If we accept there must be a First Cause, or Grand Designer, or that God must exist because we can think of him, this does not give us any proof that the god which exists is the God of the Bible or the Qur'an, or of any other specific religious tradition. This is precisely the problem with Pascal's pragmatic wager.

For an adherent of one of the standard main European religions – Christianity, Judaism and Islam – there is no argument to be had about belief in God or, particularly, about his nature. For other philosophers, though, this has been an issue.

ARGUMENTS FOR RELIGIOUS TOLERANCE
Writing in Letters Concerning Toleration *(1689–92), the English philosopher and physician John Locke (1632–1704)*

> *gave three reasons for religious tolerance. First, mortal humans can't dependably evaluate the claims of different religions. Secondly, even if we could be sure of a true religion, belief cannot be compelled; the best that regulation can do is produce token compliance with a heavy burden of resentment. Thirdly, coercion would lead to more discord and violence than would tolerance.*

What is God like?

Thales of Miletus sought a naturalistic explanation for the observable world, but still believed that God is the mind of the world and infuses all things. Xenophanes (*c*.570–*c*.475BC) believed there was a single deity that was 'in no way like men in shape or in thought' but 'caused all things by the thought of his mind'.

These depictions of God are clearly not the same as the Homeric gods – a bunch of anthropomorphized and often churlish or vindictive deities who meddled in human affairs and had sex with humans at every opportunity. The Ancient Greek philosopher Epicurus (341–270BC) also rejected the idea of interventionist gods. He left the first discussion of 'the problem of evil', asking:

> *'Is God willing to prevent evil, but not able? Then he is not omnipotent. Is he able, but not willing? Then he is malevolent. Is he both able and willing? Then how can there be evil?'*

Epicurus concluded the gods had no interest in human affairs.

Around 500 years later, the Egyptian-born philosopher Plotinus (*c*.AD204–270) reinterpreted Plato's writings in a way that put a tripartite divinity at the centre. This made him – and through him, Plato – immediately accessible to Christian tradition and made tenable Plato's position as an acceptable pagan in Christian theology. Plotinus is considered the father of neoplatonism. For centuries, Plato was known principally through Plotinus.

THE FIRST TRINITY

Plotinus' trinity comprised the One, the Intellect and the Soul. Unlike the Christian trinity, these are not of equal standing but are successive 'stages' of contemplative being. The One, sometimes called 'the Good', is beyond description and is the mystical, ineffable source of reality. Everything emanates from the One. Plotinus believed we could achieve union with the One or ultimate Being by means of contemplation. The Intellect is the 'Nous', which corresponds to the divine mind or reason, and is the first thing to emanate from the One. From this comes the World Soul, and from that individual souls and then matter. Everything, then, is in a hierarchical chain of creation extending downwards from the One, but everything at the same time is part of the One, having come from it.

The spread of Christianity and then Islam rather put an end to questions about the nature of God for more than a thousand years. Then, in the Age of Enlightenment, thinkers such as Spinoza and Voltaire challenged the prevailing dogma and the nature of God was again up for debate. The question raised by Pascal's wager – which God to bet on – opened out from a matter of choosing between different flavours of Judeo-Christian religion or Islam into also offering the pantheistic, Geist-style God described by Spinoza. This God was not tied to any existing doctrine and didn't have any interest in human affairs. In a way, it's a philosopher's God rather than a believer's God. There is no point in praying to or worshipping a god who is not interventionist or even interested. Such a deity doesn't answer Kierkegaard's need for an 'idea for which I can live and die', and doesn't provide the foundation of a moral code or social structure. But such a deity is exempt from the one crucial question that challenges philosophers who defend the existence of a supposedly benign, interventionist God – the existence of evil.

GOD AND EVIL

The problem of evil – how it can exist in a world created and overseen by an infinitely powerful and benign deity – was first raised by Epicurus writing 2,300 years ago. The problem of suffering is similar, but simpler in philosophical terms. Suffering can be explained as part of a bigger plan that we can't understand, or as a precursor to greater rewards after death. But

James Gillray's 1790 cartoon depicts the 'Atheistical-Revolutionist' Richard Price. He was deemed 'atheistical' because he was a Unitarian (he denied the tripartite nature of God) and a 'revolutionist' because he supported American independence.

why would an infinitely good God allow the existence of evil – or even create evil? Here are some of the answers philosophers have suggested:

Irenaeus (*c.*AD125–202) said that without evil in the world it would not be possible for us to achieve moral good and love for God. The existence of evil is necessary for building our souls.

St Augustine argued that the occurrence of evil is a result of the Fall, but that evil does not exist *per se* – it is a deviance from or absence of good, just as blindness is not 'something' but is rather a lack of sight. Adam and Eve chose to defy God and so chose not to be good. Others can make the same choice.

St Thomas Aquinas largely followed Augustine, adding that evil does not exist as an objective fact but as a subjective judgement. Things are only evil when judged in relation to other events, things or people. All things are innately good but may incidentally produce evil results, so the cause of all things – even evil – is good: 'This is part of the infinite goodness of God, that He should allow evil to exist, and out of it produce good.'

The religious reformers Martin Luther (1483–1546) and John Calvin (1509–64) both explained evil as the result of the Fall of Man. Both also believed in predestination, so the Fall was an inevitable part of God's plan (as were all subsequent evils). God's plan is not understandable by humankind.

Gottfried Leibniz (1646–1716), best known as a mathematician, argued that God has created the best possible world so any flaws are inevitable in all possible worlds. He claimed that moral and physical evil (sin and suffering respectively) are the result of imperfect humans operating with incomplete understanding and exercising their free will in a sub-optimal manner. Some evil is necessary to make the 'best possible' world, as virtues such as courage and morality do not have meaning or even exist if there is no danger or evil as their counterpoint. God has to balance good and evil to get the 'best possible' solution.

The British cleric Thomas Malthus (1766–1834) argued that evil exists to spur humankind to hard work and virtuous behaviour as a way of escaping hunger and poverty: 'Evil exists in the world not to create despair, but activity.'

Debate about the problem of evil continues. People of faith are often satisfied with the 'it's a mystery' line, but for philosophy that's not good enough. The best solutions seem to be either that there is no God or that the definition of God is wrong – he is not both infinitely good and infinitely powerful. But then that means 'God', as we have defined him, doesn't exist and either something else does or nothing does.

THE BEST OF ALL POSSIBLE WORLDS

Leibniz's theory of the best of all possible worlds was the butt of Voltaire's satirical novel Candide *(1759). In it, the naïve youth Candide meets a devastating string of catastrophes with blithe stoicism, putting his trust in the lesson of his tutor Pangloss that he is living in the best of all possible worlds. But the degree of suffering to which Candide and his companions are subjected is too extreme for him to hold fast to this belief. Eventually he is disillusioned and resigned to spending his remaining days tending his vegetable garden.*

CHAPTER 3
What is it to be human?

'*What a piece of work is a man! how Noble in Reason? how infinite in faculty? in form and moving how express and admirable? in Action, how like an Angel? in apprehension, how like a God? the beauty of the world, the Paragon of Animals; and yet to me, what is this Quintessence of Dust?*'
William Shakespeare, *Hamlet* (1599–1602)

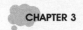

'Thou art the thing itself:
unaccommodated man is no more but such a poor bare,
forked animal as thou art.'
William Shakespeare, *King Lear* (1603–06)

What are you? A mind? A body? A mind and a body? A mind in a body? Do you exist at all? Why do you exist?

Do I/you exist?

Many philosophers have rooted existence in consciousness. To be conscious of our existence is then deemed to be sufficient proof of it, as we have to exist in some form in order to be thinking about whether or not we exist. Aristotle wrote that 'to be conscious that we are perceiving or thinking is to be conscious that we exist'. St Augustine pointed out that we can't argue we don't exist, because just having the argument proves us wrong – what is not there cannot argue.

The Muslim philosopher Ibn Sīnā, born in what is now Uzbekistan, devised a thought experiment while in prison. Known as the 'floating man', it proposed that if a man came into being, suddenly, suspended in air with no sensory input from anything including his own body, he would still be aware and able to think. Avicenna's conclusion was that the very act of thinking and being self-conscious would prove to the man that he existed. In addition, the thought experiment shows that the mind or soul is separate from the body as it can act without any inter-relationship with the body. The floating man/mind's first awareness would be of its own existence, or its essence. This self clearly doesn't depend on a physical body; therefore, the mind and body are separate and the mind is immaterial.

The most famous statement of the proof of existence is René Descartes' *cogito ergo sum*: 'I think, therefore I am' (and, more fully, 'I doubt, therefore I think, therefore I am'). It is very close to the position taken by Aristotle and Augustine, but Descartes' version is snappier as a sound bite. Kant's extrapolation of the same argument is more long-winded, but says the same.

Even with all these authoritative philosophers and common sense coming down on the side of human existence, there have been those who have doubted the proof of it. Some critics point out that thinking only proves that the 'I' thinks, but not that the 'I' exists. As the Finnish philosopher Jaakko Hintikka (born 1929) has pointed out, if the statement were wrong, we would be left with an impossibility: 'I don't exist, but I'm still wrong' – you can't be wrong if you don't exist. The French philosopher Pierre Gassendi (1592–1655) pointed out that thinking only demonstrates the existence of the thinking itself – that the thinking is happening. Friedrich Nietzsche, Søren Kierkegaard and David Hume all made the same point. It is too big a leap to assume the existence of the 'I' that Descartes is laying claim to. Recognizing the existence of thoughts is not evidence that one is a particular thinker – the thinker of 'I think, therefore I am' could as easily be a tadpole as Descartes, and he might be wholly deluded in his sense of personal identity.

But Kierkegaard's argument was not that Descartes didn't exist, but that the logic was a bit circular. We have to presuppose a thinker exists to do any thinking, so taking the thinking as evidence of existence is not acceptable. The question comes back to what the 'I' is. What or who are you?

> 'The reality of external objects does not admit of strict proof. On the contrary, however, the reality of the object of our internal sense (of myself and state) is clear immediately through consciousness.'
> Immanuel Kant, *The Critique of Pure Reason* (1781)

21 GRAMS

An American physician, Dr Duncan McDougall (1866–1920), attempted to discover the weight of the human soul. He weighed six elderly patients who were dying of tuberculosis and recorded an average weight loss at death of 21 grams. After conducting the same experiment with sheep, he claimed to see a slight increase in weight, and then a decrease – a result he explained by suggesting that a soul-portal arrived just before the departure of the soul and this briefly added to the mass of the body. The same experiment with dogs produced no variation in mass. McDougall concluded from this that the human soul weighs around 21 grams and that dogs have no souls (although presumably sheep do). His findings are not considered reliable.

Body and spirit

It must have occurred to people very early on that there is a distinct difference between dead people and living people. In dead people, something has disappeared. They are no longer animated (from *anima*, meaning spirit). They are lacking a soul, or whatever it is we decide makes a person a living, thinking being. For thousands of years, people have made up stories or used religion to explain where the 'being' part of dead people goes to; perhaps it re-joined some universal One or perhaps it hung around somehow, as a useful ancestor-spirit that might be able to intervene on behalf of the living. Perhaps it retained its personal integrity and moved on to another realm. Perhaps it was recycled, appearing in some new body, whether human or another creature. Or perhaps, most dismally, it just disappeared into nothingness. The dualism of mind and body, in various forms, emerged in cultures around the world and has been a persistent feature of religion and philosophy.

Religion thrives on the separation between the body and some kind of insubstantial soul or mind – the spirit being variously in control of the shell it inhabits or forced into sinful behaviour by the body's depraved cravings. For philosophy, this raises various points of debate including where we should locate what we call 'I', and whether knowledge is more reliably arrived at through the physical senses or non-physical reason.

> *'What is it that, when present in a body, makes it living? –*
> *A soul.'*
>
> Plato, *Phaedo*

THE MIND/BODY PROBLEM

The mind/body problem is essentially this: what is the relationship between the mind and the body (or between physical and mental phenomena)? It is clear that there seem to be two sorts of state: physical and mental. Physical states are public – we can all see if someone is fat or thin, tall or short, for instance. Mental states are private – we can't tell what someone else is thinking or feeling (though we might gather clues from physical signs). Other questions spring from the overarching mind/body question: what are physical and mental states? How can the mind affect the body and vice versa? What am 'I' or where is 'I', the person I think of as myself – mind or body? What is consciousness and how is it related to mind and body?

There are, broadly, three types of approach. The physicalist or materialist view is that everything is a physical state, even the mind. Idealists say all things are mental (for example, we construct the reality we experience). Dualists say that both physical and mental are real.

ONE, TWO OR THREE PARTS?

In *Phaedo*, Plato considered humans to comprise three components: a soul, a mind and a body. The soul is part of the Universal Being and is immortal. While we are alive, it is trapped in the body, along with the mind. The mind strives towards knowledge of the ideal Forms but the body is drawn to mundane sensual pleasures. It is the soul's job to try to guide body and mind to work together, like a charioteer trying to steer a chariot by commanding two horses. It's a challenging task and rarely successful, so most people live lives that are dominated by their physical needs and desires.

For Plato, the soul is not material, and is not destroyed by death. Instead, it returns to the Universal Being and is later reincarnated in another being. It seems that this was not standard thinking before Plato; the audience to Socrates' pronouncements on the soul in *Phaedo* were surprised he said that the soul did not dissipate at the death of the body, like breath or smoke.

NESTED SOULS OF DIFFERENT RATINGS

For Plato's pupil, Aristotle, the soul was the part of a being that was causally responsible for its animate activities. Aristotle saw a hierarchy of three types of soul, with the higher levels encompassing the lower levels. The most basic provides only the capabilities for nutrition and reproduction, the next level also provides for locomotion and perception, and the highest-ranking soul also has the capacity for thought. A bargain-basement soul could animate a plant; a medium-grade soul could animate an animal; but a human needs a high-grade soul.

Aristotle saw the soul as inseparably linked with the body; it is what gives the body capacity to do things. The soul could not, in his view, survive the body's death, nor is it individuated in any interesting way. We each have separate souls as we are separate people, but all our souls are pretty much the same, just as each person's bones are pretty much the same. So, although the soul is a different kind of material from the body, it is not an ethereal thing that could continue in independent existence, be recycled, or be held responsible for the virtuousness or otherwise of the ensouled individual.

For Aristotle, matter did not have properties of its own that were separate from the soul. How matter behaves depends on the Form it is in, and the Form is given by the soul. One hunk of meat might be a human, another hunk of meat might be an antelope – the material constituents are the same, but the soul (Form) is different.

ONLY SLIGHTLY SOULISH

Epicurus took an even more physicalist view. He followed Democritus (*c*.460–370BC) in believing that all matter consists of very tiny particles or atoms. The atoms of the soul, he said, were more agile than those of the body, but they were just as much physical entities. He made one important modification to Democritus' theory, though. According to Epicurus, atoms originally moved in parallel lines in the void but some, by an act of free will, swerved and bumped into others. These collisions gave rise to the different types of matter in the universe. (With the exception of the parallel lines, this is essentially the same position as modern physics – hydrogen atoms colliding produce first helium and then, in further combinations, other elements.) Extending his model to humans, Epicurus saw the soul as nothing more than the movement of atoms in the material body, but with the soul atoms freely swerving around. This unexplained property of atomic free will led to the free will that humans enjoy.

*In Byzantine iconography, the soul is
depicted as a bird trapped in a cage.
The bird outside the cage has
been liberated by death.*

These three classical philosophers demonstrate that there is already a spectrum of theories about souls which ranges from an immortal soul distinct from the body, to something entirely physical and with only slight differences in form from the body. Although we no longer share Epicurus' view of the way matter works, his theory finds its modern counterpart in the belief that all thought, intentionality and personality come about only through the physical and chemical processes of neurology. Or, as French philosopher Maurice Merleau-Ponty put it in the 20th century: 'I am my body.'

THE NEOPLATONIC SOUL
The beliefs of the ancients in this matter, as in so many others, filtered through to medieval and then Renaissance Europe in the writings of Plotinus and the early translators. Plotinus, as usual, adapted a Platonic view and took a tripartite approach, with the One at the top, the Intellect coming next, and the Soul placed below it. The Soul has two aspects: one that looks upwards or inwards towards the divine by means of the Intellect, and the other, outward-looking aspect that is Nature. Nature is responsible for the material world; the Soul corresponds to rational thought. The Intellect is the source of the archetypes or Platonic 'Forms' and, in its realm, there is no distinction between thought and object, perceiver and perceived. Plotinus likens the Intellect to the light

of the Sun: it illuminates the One, and is the means by which the One contemplates itself. Both levels of Soul are present in humans and it is up to us whether we are preoccupied with the lower, bodily concerns of Nature or devote our attention to the higher-level realities of the Intellect.

These three levels of reality, the One, the Intellect and the Soul, are levels of contemplation of a singular, eternal reality, not a progression through time. Nature creates time as a kind of fudge because it can't contemplate the divine. According to Plotinus, time comes about only in the lower order of existence because the Soul can't contemplate the ideal Forms directly, but only fragmented in objects perceived in a sequence of moments.

God kidnaps body and soul

With the emergence and growth of Christianity in Europe, the body and soul took on slightly different and more fixed forms. Thomas Aquinas, mediating as usual between Aristotle and

William Blake's 1808 depiction of the soul departing the body shows two distinct entities.

71

Christian doctrine, took the Aristotelian model of the body consisting of both matter and Form with the soul providing the Form. But in keeping with Christian thought, he rejected Aristotle's idea that the body and soul were equally corruptible and dissipated on death. The Church taught that the soul survives death and is immortal.

Aquinas did not, however, think the soul was pretty much the same as the person but without the body. He maintained that on the death of the body the personality and memories of the human concerned are lost. Aquinas followed contemporary Christian teaching in considering that on the Day of Judgement the body and soul would be reunited to form a whole person.

The 'ghost in the machine'

Perhaps the most famous account of the split between the body and soul is so-called Cartesian dualism. René Descartes believed that there are only two sorts of substance: mind and matter. (God was not considered to be any kind of substance.) These two substances have their own distinguishing characteristics. For matter, it is its physical extension in space – 'thereness', we could say. For mind, it is the activity of thinking.

> 'But what then am I? A thing that thinks. What is that?
> A thing that doubts, understands, affirms, denies, wills,
> refuses, and which also imagines and senses.'
>
> René Descartes, Meditations (1641)

Descartes argued that while the body is divisible, the mind is not. We can lose a leg, and our body still survives and exists, but we cannot have half a mind, or half a thought. John Locke tried to counter this by saying that when we are unconscious or asleep the mind is discontinuous. This is not much of an argument, as Locke was citing discontinuity through time, whereas Descartes was talking about spatial divisibility.

Matter follows deterministic rules – it can't act at random. That physical laws govern the material universe was one of the defining discoveries of Descartes' age, and his own work on mathematics was part of it. The physical body, then, must work according to rules. Descartes came to see the body as a machine, controlled by the mind. But how would the mind, which has no substance, interact with the body, pulling the levers, as it were, to make it do things? Descartes decided that there must be an organ which enabled this interaction and he chose the pineal gland – a small structure buried deep in the brain.

Descartes' model of how the mind and body interact. Light from an object travels to the eyes, where information is conveyed to the pineal gland, the part of the body that he believed was responsible for mediating between mind and matter. An instruction to move the hand can be initiated by the pineal gland.

‍

> '*I am present to my body not merely in the way a seaman is present to his ship, but . . . I am tightly joined and, so to speak, mingled together with it, so much so that I make up one single thing with it.*'
>
> René Descartes, *Meditations* (1641)

INDUBITABILITY – A NIFTY TRICK

Descartes had a way of testing his ideas by thinking about which things he could doubt and about which things he felt secure. He decided he could not doubt the existence of his mind, but he could doubt the existence of his body (he might just imagine it). As those things he doubted must be different from those things he did not doubt, it followed that mind and body must be different things.

GOD GETS IN ON THE ACT

Even locating the mind (or soul) in an organ does not deal with the mechanism of interaction. If the mind and body are different, with the mind utterly distinct from corporeal things, how, then, can one have any causal effect on the other? Clearly, our minds and bodies interact in some way: trapping a finger in a door makes us feel pain; when we choose to carry out a physical action, our bodies respond.

To solve the dilemma, the French philosopher Nicolas Malebranche (1638–1715) brought God in on the act – literally. God, Malebranche claimed, is the only causal power. The individual mind is a limited shadow of the one universal mind which is God. Our minds have no power to cause anything in the physical world.

Nor do physical objects have the power to affect other physical objects, since in order to cause something to happen it's necessary to know how to cause it. In every case, God acts as an intermediary, causing a willed action to happen. This demands a lot of God, as He has to pay attention to everyone at all times, controlling every aspect of their lives. The mind and body are like two clocks, wound up by God and kept in time with each other by divine acts. This is the doctrine of occasionalism.

Although occasionalism seems to solve the problem of mind–body interaction, it has its own problems, not the least of which is the existence of God. Hume – who didn't believe in God anyway – mocked it as ridiculous, saying that if we can't even say how the human mind works, who are we to guess at how God's mind works?

DENYING DUALISM

A thoroughly materialist view, in which the mind is seen purely as a product or aspect of the physical brain, solves the dualist problem by denying dualism. Spinoza's view was that mind and body are simply different ways of looking at parts of a single all-encompassing and homogenous whole. This removes the problem by denying the separate existence of mind and body. The German philosopher Friedrich Schelling (1775–1854) came to a similar conclusion by a roundabout and confusing method that even Hegel had difficulty understanding, denouncing it as 'All . . . a tangled mass of abstractions.'

Hume took issue with Descartes' claim of indivisibility, saying there is no reason to suppose that we have a unity, rather than a diversity, of thought or perception. We have lots of thoughts, dreams and perceptions, so under what pretext can we lump them all together and say the mind is indivisible? Rather than the self being a thinking thing, it is no more than a bundle of perceptions. Even the term 'bundle' implies a grouping together into some sort of unity.

Immanuel Kant replied to this argument by saying it is necessary to presuppose an ego (a self) to do the perceiving, otherwise the collection of 'sense-data' which we interpret as seeing a tree or hearing the wind would just remain uninterpreted data – it would have no meaning. Kant pointed out that the mind could deteriorate and there was no reason to suppose it could not or did not die with the body.

Gilbert Ryle (1900–76), who coined the term 'the ghost in the machine' for Descartes' model of the mind piloting the body, dismissed dualism as a 'category mistake'. Ryle said that mind and body are the same thing and there is in fact no gap between mental acts and behaviours. Feelings are manifest in behaviour; the apparent separateness of feelings is only a construct of language which comes about purely because of the way we use language to describe what is happening. He noted that in dualist discourse the mind is always described in negative terms: non-physical, non-spatial, non-temporal, non-observable. If the body is clockwork, the mind is 'not bits of clockwork . . . just bits of nonclockwork'. He also observed that when we talk about mental or emotional states, what we are actually describing is a tendency to behave in a certain way. If we say someone is angry or sad, we expect or anticipate certain behaviours of them that demonstrate those emotions – we don't directly comprehend any inner state.

CATEGORY ERROR

The term category mistake or category error was introduced by Gilbert Ryle in 1949. It describes the way in which someone may misidentify an object or concept. An example would be to say there are three things in a field: two cows, and a pair of cows. Another would be to show someone all the buildings that make up a university – libraries, sports facilities, student housing – and then have them ask where the university itself is. The visitor's mistake is to presume that the university belongs to the category 'physical infrastructure' rather than the category 'institution'.

Are you now who you were before?

Wherever we think our identity is located, whether in a separate mind or in 'bundles of perceptions', we all feel we are someone. Defining that someone and pinning it down can be difficult. The self is a slippery thing, prone to changing through time and with experience. In what ways do we stay the same person?

In *An Essay Concerning Human Understanding* (1689), John Locke proposed that it is the continuity of consciousness which determines identity. He did not root identity or continuity

in the body or even in the soul: he said someone could be the re-incarnation of Plato but would not be Plato, having no continuity of consciousness with Plato. It is on the basis of continuing consciousness, in the form of remembering what we have done and having enduring feelings and personality traits, that we can be said to remain the same person and therefore be held accountable for acts we have committed in the past.

The English philosopher John Locke set out to investigate the mechanisms of human thought and understanding.

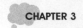

> '[The self is] that conscious thinking thing (whatever substance, made up of whether spiritual, or material, simple, or compounded, it matters not) which is sensible, or conscious of pleasure and pain, capable of happiness or misery, and so is concerned for itself, as far as that consciousness extends.'
>
> John Locke, *An Essay Concerning Human Understanding* (1689)

Hume, with his 'bundle of perceptions' theory, had no place to locate the self. He believed the parts of the soul or consciousness are a commonwealth or loose collection of perceptions, thoughts, memories and opinions. Hume even said that personal identity is a fiction. He noted in the appendix to his *Treatise on Human Nature* (1739–40) that he was dissatisfied with his account of the self – but never returned to it.

The Scottish philosopher Thomas Reid (1710–96) challenged Locke's account of personal identity being rooted in continuity through time with his 'brave officer' argument:

> '*Suppose a brave officer to have been flogged when a boy at school for robbing an orchard, to have taken a standard from the enemy in his first campaign, and to have been made a general in advanced life; suppose, also, which must be admitted to be possible, that, when he took the standard, he was conscious of his having been flogged at school, and that, when made a general, he was conscious of his taking the standard, but had absolutely lost the consciousness of his flogging.*'

According to Locke, the general must be the same person as the brave officer, and the brave officer must be the same person as the boy. But as there is no psychological connection between the general and the boy, they are not the same person. The strength of the argument lies in showing that Locke's position results in a contradiction, because the general both is and is not the same person as the boy who was flogged at school. The transitivity of identity is the principle that if A = B and B = C then A = C. But Locke's criterion of personal identity contradicts this rule; his criterion as either a necessary or sufficient condition of identity must be rejected.

THESEUS' SHIP

The Greek historian Plutarch described a paradox relating to a ship owned by Theseus. As parts of the ship wore out, they were replaced with new wood. Eventually, none of the original parts remained. Was it still the same ship?

Versions of the paradox referring to different objects have proliferated. The paradox can be applied to the human body: during the course of our lives, our cells are replaced over and over so that we are literally not the same person in terms of our physical being – yet we consider ourselves to be the same.

The rise of the individual

Defining human identity in terms of either the mechanics of the body or its partaking of a great universal spirit does not accord with our personal experience of our identity. A revolt against these methods – both of which appear reductionist in different ways – began towards the end of the 18th century. The French-

Swiss philosopher Jean-Jacques Rousseau (1712–78), and the German philosophers Arthur Schopenhauer (1788–1860) and Friedrich Nietzsche were among those who felt that human consciousness cannot be reduced either to parts of a body operating mechanically, or to a little parcel of an all-inclusive godhead or natural spirit.

What has become known as the Romantic movement tried to pull humankind out of the squalid, technology-oriented drudgery into which the Industrial Revolution had driven it and to reclaim the individual in philosophy. Nature and art were both considered the true home of the human spirit, the source of uplifting and liberating self-realization. The strong passions of the individual – the striving of the self, the passionate involvement with others, with nature and with God – were put at the centre of the human experience.

CHILDHOOD: NURTURING THE NEW INDIVIDUAL

Rousseau wrote some of the most important treatises on education and society of his time – perhaps of all time. He felt that the perfect condition of humans could be realized if allowed to flourish from childhood. His ideas on personal freedoms and social responsibilities lay at the heart of the French Revolution and the American Declaration of Independence.

It was Rousseau's belief that humankind was innately good and moral, but that these qualities had been overlaid and corrupted by the nature of contemporary society. He advocated more natural (and universal) education, with children taught morality initially and intellectual disciplines later on. In particular, education in religion should wait until the child was 18 years old and had developed critical faculties. Rousseau was not in favour of indoctrination or unexamined beliefs.

For Rousseau, contemporary society, industrialization, greed and science had all formed a crust of corruption over the

The spirit of the Romantic movement is captured in this painting entitled Wanderer Above the Sea of Fog *by Caspar David Friedrich. Its message of Kantian self-reflection suggests the human, in contemplation of nature, as noble and triumphant but also insignificant against the vastness of the natural world.*

natural nobility of humankind. A simpler life, closer to nature and focused on feeling and compassion, was the way for people to realize their potential and live the life they were born for. His two most important works, *The Social Contract* and *Émile*, were both published in 1762.

In *Émile*, he outlines a plan for the ideal education of a young person. He felt the process should be child-centred. The child should be brought up in the countryside, working under the guidance of a tutor who would allow him or her to experiment in a safe environment. Early education should be concerned with emotions, with rational subjects not introduced until the age of 12. Rousseau argued that there was no virtue in the usual method of education, which required the child to use reason early on. If children could reason, Rousseau argued, they would not need to be educated. He also advocated that young adults learn a practical skill, such as carpentry, both for the benefits it offered and as a back-up in case of a change in their fortunes.

The German writer Johann Wolfgang von Goethe (1749–1832) is best known as a literary figure in the Romantic movement, but his work also had a significant effect on philosophy. One of Goethe's recurring themes was the tension between the passionate individual and the strictures of society. One of the people he influenced was Schopenhauer, perhaps the most pessimistic philosopher of all time.

ENSLAVED BY THE WILL

While Rousseau's view of human potential was highly optimistic, Schopenhauer saw the exact opposite. He regarded people as eternally hobbled by the driving force of the Will, a universal and perpetual striving that trapped and enslaved each individual. Along with Kant, Schopenhauer considered the phenomenal (physical world) to be an illusion. He believed that reality – the 'thing-in-itself' – was actually the Will, which manifested in all phenomena and beings because it has an insatiable urge to reveal itself in the world. We are all at the mercy of the Will, enslaved by its demands, and it is the cause of all our suffering. Schopenhauer believed that the Will is revealed to the subjective self immediately and non-conceptually, though he never really explains what comprises this immediate awareness. It is hard to imagine just how gloomy the Schopenhauerian scenario is: he considered the world to be hell, with people playing the part both of damned souls and tormenting demons.

Schopenhauer felt that the way to escape from suffering was to conquer the Will and free ourselves from its rule. We can overcome it through contemplation of the arts (particularly music), through compassion and through religious contemplation and asceticism.

Art and music allow us to contemplate the universal Will separated from our own individual strivings, allowing a measure of objectivity. Compassionate engagement with another person leads us to recognize ourselves in them and them in us, and quietens the clamouring of the Will. The best source of peace, though, is religious fulfilment. A life of asceticism and meditation, denying the Will, leads to a blissful contemplation of nothingness. (Schopenhauer was the first Western philosopher to be heavily influenced by Eastern religions.)

Schopenhauer maintained that recognizing our enslavement leads us to the realization that we should not fear death. We need to overcome the Will's desire to exist in the world of appearances, which gives rise to our individual existence and, consequently, our suffering. Schopenhauer's argument seems to favour suicide in order to thwart the Will's evil plan. He tries to avoid this conclusion by claiming that as suicide is an act of Will it constitutes a surrender of the intellect: it is better, therefore, to defeat the Will through contemplation.

> 'To our amazement we suddenly exist, after having for countless millennia not existed; in a short while we will again not exist, also for countless millennia. That cannot be right, says the heart.'
>
> Arthur Schopenhauer,
> *The World as Will and Idea* (1819)

Nietzsche was greatly influenced by Schopenhauer, but did not share his extreme pessimism about humankind's destiny. Nietzsche saw the Will not as a slave-master but as a strong force which could propel humans to greatness if allowed to achieve fulfilment. His concept of the *Übermensch* – 'superman' or 'beyond-man' – is similar to Aristotle's man of virtue. The *Übermensch* is the psychically strong human, not bowed down by the 'moral slavery' of Christianity, who can forge new ideals and values by which humankind can hope to step forward into a brave new world.

A LIFE DISTORTED

Friedrich Nietzsche was born near Leipzig, Prussia (now in Germany), in 1844. His father, a Lutheran minister, died in 1849 and his baby brother died the following year. Nietzsche, his mother and sister went to live with his father's parents. In 1864, while studying theology, Nietzsche lost his faith and turned instead to philology (the study of language). He became interested in philosophy after reading the works of Schopenhauer in 1865 and consequently embarked on his own studies. After a brief spell in the army, he was offered a professorship at the University of Basel when he was only 24. He gave up his Prussian citizenship when he moved to Switzerland to take up his new post and remained stateless for the rest of his life.

In 1879, ill health forced Nietzsche to give up his academic post. He spent the next ten years as an independent author travelling around Europe. In 1889 he suffered a mental breakdown and remained severely mentally ill until his death in 1900.

Nietzsche became world-famous during the later years of his life, but his reputation was tarnished by the actions of his sister, who used his writings to further the Nazi cause.

Friedrich Nietzsche was one of the most profound and enigmatic philosophers in history. Unfortunately, he has also become one of the most controversial because of the way in which his ideas were invoked and exploited by the Nazis.

Elisabeth had split with her brother after marrying a man who held extreme anti-Semitic views. She moved with him to Paraguay to form Nueva Germania, intended as a model community built on the virtues of German culture and society. The colony was not a success. Her husband committed suicide and Elisabeth returned to Germany in 1893, where she slowly took control of her brother's literary legacy. Her corrupted version of Nietzsche's unfinished The Will to Power *was later used, with Elisabeth's blessing, as evidence that Nietzsche sympathized with views later espoused by the Nazis. In fact, he did not. Nietzsche was not a fan of anything German and thought the term 'German culture' was a contradiction in terms. When Elisabeth died in 1935, Adolf Hitler attended her funeral. Through his sister's actions, Nietzsche's philosophy was brought into a state of disrepute from which it has still not fully recovered.*

The *Übermensch* that Nietzsche described in *Thus Spoke Zarathustra* (1883–85) is a goal humanity can set for itself so that future generations will be superior. It's easy to see how this idea could be distorted by a regime that dreamed of a superior, elite master-race. The Nazis appropriated Nietzsche's term *Übermensch* and introduced their own term, *Untermensch* (one never used by Nietzsche) for the underclass which could rightly (in their view) be enslaved or destroyed.

'*O brave new world,
That has such people in't.*'
William Shakespeare, *The Tempest* (1610–11)

THE PERSONAL PERSON

Kierkegaard thought about the individual in a much more personal way. He rejected Descartes' dualism and felt that arguing about whether reason or experience offered a better way of making sense of the world was to miss the point, as neither takes account of the nature of a human being and the fundamental human condition. He was critical of Hegel and Goethe and felt it was the task of philosophy to address how each person can live 'as an individual'. He saw humankind at each juncture as facing choices, having to make decisions, and lacking a way of making them. The quotation with which we started the book, as an explanation of the point of philosophy, was for Kierkegaard a statement of the dilemma of being human:

> 'What I really lack is to be clear in my mind what I am
> to do, not what I am to know . . . the thing is to find a
> truth which is true for me, to find the idea for which I
> can live and die.'

This burden, which emerged repeatedly as a theme in Kierkegaard's writing, was also recognized by the existentialists. Kierkegaard has sometimes been called the first existentialist and, certainly, in *The Concept of Anxiety* (1844), he dealt with the angst created by our awareness that we have freedom to act, choices to make, but no guiding principle to help us. He developed a theory of three stages or competing life philosophies. The aesthetic is preoccupied with the here and now, with current pleasures and problems, and lacks commitment to anything greater. Despair follows when the aesthetic discovers the emptiness of such a life. The ethical person recognizes the importance of ideals, but is inevitably consumed with guilt when unable to live up to his or her own standards.

Kierkegaard had an answer, but one which the most ardent existentialists would reject: religion. His third stage, the religious,

WHAT IS IT TO BE HUMAN?

sees the individual wholly committed to transcendent ideals. Kierkegaard took religious belief to be an act not of reason but of faith. He saw faith as the opposite of reason, since if religious truths can be explained then there is no place for faith. For him, religion was an intensely personal thing, with God coming to each individual in an appropriate way.

> 'Each age has its characteristic depravity. Ours is perhaps not pleasure or indulgence or sensuality, but rather a dissolute pantheistic contempt for individual man.'
>
> Søren Kierkegaard

Nietzsche is often considered the greatest of the Romantics, but as the 19th century gave way to the 20th it was not optimism that flourished as the legacy of the Romantic movement. The dour gloom of Schopenhauer and the confusion of Kierkegaard looking for a beacon in the confusion of angst laid a path towards existentialism – the movement that seized on the concept of humankind's essential solitude and hopeless search for meaning.

> '[Nietzsche] had a more penetrating knowledge of himself than any other man who ever lived or was ever likely to live.'
>
> Sigmund Freud, founder of psychoanalysis

Edging towards existentialism

While Kierkegaard had prepared the ground for existentialism, it was Martin Heidegger who planted the seed. In many ways, it was a natural follow-up to Romanticism, especially after

Freud's insights into how the individual self is shaped by personal experiences, and the erosion of universal religious belief. Heidegger's insistence that we have to forge a life while facing our mortality marked a major turning point in 20th-century philosophy. His *Being and Time*, published in 1927, had a huge impact on later thinkers in many spheres, most notably on the development of existentialism under Jean-Paul Sartre and deconstructionist criticism under the Algerian-French philosopher Jacques Derrida (1930–2004).

EXISTENCE BEFORE EXISTENTIALISM

The origins of existentialism lie in Heidegger's enquiries into *Dasein*, the 'being that we ourselves are' or – literally translated – 'being-there'.

Heidegger saw *Dasein* as a self-conscious entity, aware of its own mutability: it knows that it is finite, mortal and will meet its inevitable fate. This awareness necessarily leads to angst or dread. But this is essential for life to have meaning. Only if we are fully aware of our limited lives can we live with authenticity and purpose. Self-awareness enables us to create a life from nothing, in the face of dread and death, referring only to purposes we have chosen for ourselves. (Heidegger's emphasis on choice is important.) It is an uncompromising and daunting view of life that has no room for a divinity offering purpose. Unlike earlier philosophers, such as St Augustine and Kierkegaard, who believed that as individuals we 'find' ourselves through God, Heidegger thought God irrelevant in philosophical terms. It is only the certain knowledge that we will die that gives our lives direction.

Human existence is defined by time, as past experiences and future hopes dictate who we are and what we do in a way that does not affect inanimate objects, because their type of existence is static.

Heidegger distinguishes between authentic and inauthentic ways of living. An authentic life is one of our own choosing, which we build for ourselves. But we are free to choose the inauthentic, and Heidegger tries to say this is not a lesser choice. Authenticity is acting in the world, being a part of it on our own terms, defining ourselves. It is difficult to achieve while the *Dasein* is immersed in the world. Luckily, anxiety (angst) is there to act as midwife. When *Dasein* is beset by existential angst, when the world suddenly seems bereft of meaning and we stare into the face of our inevitable demise, the world recedes. Then it is possible to be free (from the world and others) and to become ourselves.

It may seem perverse that the certainty of death is what frees us to make our lives. But imagine you found an elixir of life that made you immortal. All your current ambitions lose their urgency. You might like to learn Arabic or become a politician. There is plenty of time, so no need to hurry; instead you decide to surf the web and dig the garden. There is no limit to the tomorrows in which you can achieve your ambitions, and no limit to the ambitions you can achieve. There is no need to choose or know which things are important to you. The time-limitedness of life is what gives it purpose; the 'freedom' to choose is forced upon us by mortality.

Although Heidegger would later deny he was an existentialist, the principal motifs of existentialism are all first introduced in *Being and Time*: the 'being there' of existence (the importance of the self-located in the world); the importance of the individual, especially in relation to the 'crowd'; a preoccupation with angst (anxiety), death, and nihilism; the assertion that science can't provide a framework for understanding what it is to be human; the locating of 'authenticity' in life in self-realization through choice. Existentialism rejects previous systems for categorizing human existence and asserts the primacy of the individual in defining ourselves – existence is more important than essence.

This sounds more complex than it is. Our individual actions define who we are because those actions are freely chosen. Our essence therefore comes from our existence (in actions) rather than being predetermined by others (in the form of labels assigned by society) or by genetics. Carrying out kind acts defines someone as a kind person. Acting cruelly defines someone as a cruel person.

Sigmund Freud (1856–1939)

Sigmund Freud was an Austrian psychologist and the founder of 'psychoanalysis'. This method is based on the belief that certain early childhood experiences are repressed by the conscious mind. Generally, these experiences are related to sexuality, but they can be any type of experience which the child thinks other people would criticize. The repressed memories later cause physiological disruptions and mental illness, and treatment involves getting the patient to revive and discuss the memories.

Freud's ideas had a massive impact on Western thought and philosophy.

Freud suggested that psychoanalysis represented a new 'Copernican revolution' and he claimed to have proven that the conscious mind, or the self, is not 'master of its own house', as rationalist and Cartesian philosophies had supposed.

BEING, IN AND FOR ITSELF

Jean-Paul Sartre, one of the leading existentialist philosophers in post-war France, drew heavily on Heidegger and Kierkegaard, but went far beyond them. In *Being and Nothingness* (1943), he produced a powerful study of consciousness. For Sartre, appearance is the only reality, and the world can be seen as an infinite series of finite appearances. There is, however, a binary distinction between unconscious being ('being-in-itself') and conscious being ('being-for-itself'). The former cannot change and is unaware of itself. The latter is aware of its own consciousness, but incomplete, and is what defines humans. For Sartre, a tree is an example of 'being-in-itself' – it is what it is, and lacks the ability to change or create its being. But, by acting in the world, a person actuates his own being. As 'being-for-itself', he does not have a predetermined essence and is forced to create himself from nothingness.

By foraying into an unknown future, a person's essence is constantly changing. For example, if he is a scientist he is not a scientist in the way that a tree is a tree. His past, present and future are subject to a series of individual choices – despite his attempts to reach self-essentialism. As the 'being-in-itself' and the 'being-for-itself' can never be synthesized, man is aware of himself as a blank canvas, a nothingness. And, as the 'being-for-itself', he is defined by its own awareness of being not 'in-itself'.

Sartre goes on to argue that human beings can only become aware of themselves when confronted with the gaze of another. This objectifying scrutiny robs us of our inherent freedom – someone viewing a person digging a ditch may reductively identify the person as a ditch-digger, for example – and it teaches us to falsely identify ourselves as 'being-in-itself'. This imposition of consciousness becomes a burden and a limitation on our freedom. If our personal, subjective view of the world is all the truth there is, our only way to assert it is to objectify the individual who objectifies us.

Sartre's logic means that each individual is totally responsible for the life he or she chooses. Sometimes an action is a response or reaction to extreme circumstances, but even a constrained choice remains a choice and an exercise of personal power. A man with a gun pointed at his head can choose whether to obey a command or be shot. The dire consequences of the choice do not deny its existence.

Martin Heidegger (1889–1976)

Martin Heidegger was perhaps the most influential philosopher of the 20th century. But he was also – at least for a time – a Nazi, a fact that has complicated the way his ideas have been received.

As a philosophy student at the University of Marburg, Heidegger was influenced by and later employed by the philosopher and mathematician Edmund Husserl (1859–1938). On Husserl's retirement, Heidegger succeeded him as professor of philosophy at the University of Freiburg in 1928. Five years later, Heidegger became rector of Freiburg and joined the National Socialist German Workers' Party, or 'Nazi' Party, speaking in support of Hitler. He resigned as rector the following year, and his relationship with Nazism became more distant, but he remained a member of the Nazi Party until it was disbanded in 1945. He was banned from teaching between 1945 and 1949 and was never allowed to resume his original professorship on account of his Nazi sympathies. Heidegger did not publicly renounce or apologize for his Nazi views though privately he referred to them as 'the greatest stupidity of my life'. It is possible

> *that while he allowed the official implementation of Nazi reforms, he secretly resisted them at least partially – there is no clear evidence either way.*

According to Sartre, the inescapable condition of human life is the requirement of choosing *something*, and accepting responsibility for the consequences. This means we are encumbered with three burdens: anguish, abandonment and despair. Accepting total responsibility in determining the future development of humanity produces an overwhelming sense of anguish and, as there is no higher power (such as God) to turn to, this leads to a sense of abandonment. Ultimately, since we repeatedly experience evidence that our powers are not up to the task, we are driven to despair.

This weighty burden need not inevitably lead to pessimism, however. Sartre says that existentialism involves a 'stern optimism' in its message that 'the destiny of man is placed within himself'. Self-deception invariably involves an attempt to evade personal responsibility, therefore the basic question posed by Sartre is whether or not we will be true to ourselves – will we be sincere or self-deceiving? Shakespeare had already touched on this idea in Hamlet's famous question: 'To be or not to be?'

EXISTING AND EXISTENTIALISM IN SOCIETY

Taking up Sartre's conviction that as individuals we are self-determining, the French philosopher Simone de Beauvoir (1908–86) explored the role that society and context must play in helping to define personhood. In *The Second Sex* (1949), she accepted that the individual is born free but pointed out that gender inevitably pushes women into particular roles that vary between societies. Each woman 'becomes' what the

Jean-Paul Sartre (centre) and Simone de Beauvoir (on his left) were part of a group of philosophers, writers and other intellectuals who regularly convened at cafés in Paris.

term 'woman' means in her own social context, whether that is domestic goddess, career woman, temptress, supermum or anything else. The female becomes a woman by accepting and living the role that society defines as appropriate for her.

Sartre would have said that acting in accordance with someone else's expectations and then blaming them for what we become is an act of 'bad faith'. But de Beauvoir insisted that 'bad faith' presupposes an awareness of the possibility of choice and the potential for freedom. Children cannot act in bad faith; their actions are constrained by parents or guardians so they don't have the freedom to choose how to be. At adolescence they reach an 'awakening' when existentialist angst takes hold. Women have, historically, been similarly constrained according to de Beauvoir; socio-economic circumstances have defined their existence and they have been unaware of the potential for freedom. Consequently, they are not acting in bad faith in becoming the women that society expects them to be.

> '*One is not born, but rather becomes, a woman.*'
> Simone de Beauvoir, *The Second Sex* (1949)

Many of the ideas expressed by de Beauvoir in *The Second Sex* and *The Ethics of Ambiguity* (1947) have become central to the modern feminist movement: that women need to reach a point at which they can recognize their own freedoms, define their own being, and free themselves from the 'enslavement' of a society whose rules and values are defined by men.

A CRISIS OF BEING

The engodded – those who accept that there is a god, whether or not they struggle with their faith – tend to be free from existential angst. Either their purpose in living is clear or it is a great mystery which they do not presume to question. But for the atheist, the question 'Why am I here?' is one that can be too hard to face. At least, the answer – 'No reason' – can be too hard to accept. The crisis of being, of knowing why we have being, is only really possible for those who don't believe in a god.

The French-Algerian writer and philosopher Albert Camus (1913–60) was an existentialist and friend of Jean-Paul Sartre in Paris, until the pair fell out in 1951. His most important work of existentialist philosophy, *The Myth of Sisyphus* (1942), deals with the theme of 'absurdity'. Camus claims that human existence is absurd as we attempt to make sense of a senseless world. He used the Greek hero Sisyphus as an illustration of the futility and hopelessness of all human endeavour. Sisyphus is condemned by

Sisyphus was condemned forever to push a boulder uphill as a punishment for his trickery.

the gods to push a boulder up a hill for all eternity, only to have it roll back down as soon as he reaches the summit. Similarly, says Camus, we all spend our lives achieving nothing.

THE ABSURD

Absurdism holds that there is no meaning in what happens in the world. It is the opposite of a belief in karma (that good things will happen to people who act well and vice versa). The absurdist holds that the world itself is amoral: anything can happen to anyone, irrespective of their moral standing or behaviour. Absurdism is not really compatible with Christian faith as it allows for no overarching, invisible purpose or direction.

The inevitable consequence of pondering the desolate pointlessness of existence is to ask, 'Why should I not commit suicide?' Camus considers that other writers and philosophers of an existentialist bent, including Husserl, Kierkegaard, Sartre and the German psychiatrist Karl Jaspers (1883–1968), have all shied away from this conclusion. Instead of keeping faith, they have tried to resolve the conflict between the rational human being and the irrational world. But this conflict cannot be resolved, and suicide is just another attempt at resolution. We are all backed into a corner. If we accept the position of absurdity, we have to accept death. If we refuse it, we live teetering on the precipice, looking into the abyss; we exist in full knowledge of our mortality and the futility of all we do in our lives. Camus advocates 'revolt' – accepting awareness of the situation without being resigned. Suicide would be a defeat, a denial of the condition of our existence. According to Camus, 'The struggle itself is enough to fill a man's heart. One must imagine Sisyphus happy.'

> *'There is only one truly serious philosophical problem, and that is suicide.'*
>
> Albert Camus, *The Myth of Sisyphus* (1942)

> *'All the labour of the ages, all the devotion, all the inspiration, all the noonday brightness of human genius, are destined to extinction in the vast death of the solar system, and the whole temple of man's achievement must inevitably be buried beneath the debris of a universe in ruins.'*
>
> Bertrand Russell (1926)

Back to the machine – but with no ghost

The removal of God or any kind of supernatural or ethereal spirit from the consideration of the human leads us back to a physicalist view – we have Descartes' machine of the body, but with no ghost to animate it. This is the position adopted by the American philosopher Daniel Dennett (born 1942). He rejects the idea that the mind is a separate, disembodied entity, arguing that all aspects of ourselves can be explained by looking at how the brain works. Personality, intellect, opinions, thoughts, dreams – everything is reducible to neurology. He describes the brain as a 'semantic engine', a mechanism for extracting meaning from the world.

Denying that there is anything inherently special or mystical in consciousness, Dennett maintains there is no quantifiable and real difference between something that *seems* conscious and something that *is* conscious – so a computer can have conscious-ness. As computers become better able to do things we currently associate only with human intelligence, the distinction between real and artificial intelligence, between genuine consciousness and mimicked consciousness, will become less and less meaningful until it has to be abandoned. Dennett has said that even thermostats have 'beliefs' about the world. A thermostat behaves on the basis of assumptions about the world that can't be distinguished from beliefs, in that they have the same effects as beliefs. Dennett sees the brain as nothing more than a very sophisticated computer, and the mind as the product of Darwinian evolution.

Dennett's view that the brain is very like a computer is refuted by another American philosopher, John Searle (born 1932), a pioneer in cognitive science. The view that computers can be conscious, which Searle terms 'strong AI' (artificial intelligence), is challenged by a thought experiment he called 'the Chinese Room' (see panel on opposite page).

Human minds are distinguished from computers, according to Searle, by intentionality. Computers are defined syntactically, in terms of formal symbol manipulation, and that, he argues, is insufficient to imply consciousness.

THE CHINESE ROOM ARGUMENT

Imagine you are in a room with an enormous rule-book which allows you to look up Chinese sentences and tells you how to respond to them in Chinese. Through a hole in the wall, someone passes a piece of paper with a question written on it in Chinese. Using the rule-book, you look up the answer, write it down in Chinese and pass it through another hole. To the people outside the room you seem to understand Chinese, whereas in fact you have no understanding of the language at all.

The Chinese Room is an analogy for artificial intelligence. The rule-book is the equivalent of a computer program which manipulates data according to a set of rules and produces answers. It can give the appearance of being intelligent, but it is not. A computer model of the mind is not actually conscious, argues Searle, just as a computer model of the digestive system cannot actually eat pizza. A computer that can model falling in love or reading a novel or getting drunk does not experience these things, but produces a simulation of the processes involved.

CONSCIOUSNESS EMERGING

So, if consciousness is not something that can be experienced by a computer, what is it exactly, and how does it emerge? In his theories about the mind and consciousness, Searle rejects Cartesian dualism – that the mind is something non-physical and separate from the body. He also rejects the views of thinkers such as Dennett, who believe that consciousness can be reduced to a series of physical processes in the brain.

Instead, Searle takes a position which he calls biological naturalism. Consciousness is an emergent property of the brain.

He uses the analogy of water to explain the idea. Wetness is an emergent property of water that is brought about by the behaviour of water molecules *en masse*. No individual molecule is 'wet'; the wetness is a feature of the whole system of molecules and the way they behave when water is in its liquid form. In the same way, one cannot point to a neuron and say 'this one is conscious'. Consciousness emerges as a result of the whole system.

Events at the micro-level – perhaps at the level of individual neurons – cause a phenomenon that at the macro-level we call consciousness. Some have seen biological naturalism as a form of dualism since micro-level properties can be objectively studied by, for example, a brain surgeon, but the brain surgeon cannot in the same way access macro-level properties such as pain, desire or joy. Searle rejects this suggestion. He stresses that consciousness is a type of physical property; it is not something separate like a kind of juice that is squirted out by the neurons. It is the state that the system is in – part of that system and inseparable from it. How it works – how micro-level behaviour creates consciousness at the macro level – is a question for the neuroscientists. But as a problem for philosophy, Searle regards it as solved.

CHAPTER 4
What can we know?

'[The soul is] a veritable prisoner
fast bound within his body...
and that instead of investigating
reality by itself and in itself it is
compelled to peer through the
bars of its prison.'
Plato, *Phaedo*

'To say something is meaningful is to say that that is how
we arrange it so; how we comprehend it to be, and what
is comprehended by you or I may not be by a cat, for
example. If a tree falls in a park and there is no-one to
hand, it is silent and invisible and nameless. And if we were
to vanish, there would be no tree at all; any meaning would
vanish along with us. Other than what the cats make of it
all, of course.'
William Fossett, *Natural States* (1754)

Outside the existence of our own minds, what can we be sure of? Do you see the colour blue in the same way that I do? Is the Sun really hot and round? Sometimes, things that look obvious are deceptive – the Sun and Moon look about the same size, for example. But methods of investigation other than the evidence of our own senses can reveal an error in our common-sense assumptions. The branch of philosophy that deals with knowledge is called epistemology.

What makes you think you know?

How can we know things? The quality of knowledge and how we can attain certainty has puzzled philosophers for 2,500 years. In brief, there are three possible ways of knowing things:

- The evidence of our senses – we know some things by experience, by the processing of sense-data such as what we see and hear. For example, you might be certain your desk exists because you can see it and touch it.
- Reason – through reasoning or a logical sequence of thoughts you might be persuaded of the truth of a proposition such as 'the area of a square increases four-fold if you double the length of the sides'.

- Innate belief – you might believe you have a soul or that God exists because you have a strongly held conviction that this is the case.

How far each of these methods can be trusted has been debated for a long time.

> ### KNOWING THAT AND KNOWING HOW
> *Philosophers distinguish between different types of knowledge:*
>
> **Knowledge that**, *or propositional knowledge, is concerned with, for example, knowing an old friend or your home town particularly well.*
> **Knowledge how** *is concerned with acquired skills, such as knowing how to multiply numbers or ride a bicycle.*
>
> *The distinction between the two types of knowledge is most clearly expressed in linguistic terms by, for example, the French – 'connaître' and 'savoir'.*

Can we be sure?

The Greek philosopher Xenophanes was the first person known to have been cautious about claims of certainty. Anticipating Socrates, he said that even if we do discover the truth we have no way of ascertaining whether what we have discovered is correct, and that things are as we think they are. Even so, philosophical inquiry is still useful. It can reveal errors and tell us what is not the case even if we can't be certain of what is the case.

Socrates, who was born in Athens in 470BC, around the time that Xenophanes died, often claimed that the only thing he could be certain of was his own ignorance. A good deal of his teaching consisted of asking his audience to give definitions of common concepts such as 'beauty' or 'piety', then showing by reasoned argument that whatever answer they had given fell down under scrutiny, turning out to be absurd or paradoxical.

Through this, Socrates intended to show how dangerous it is to accept established ideas uncritically. He frequently demolished in argument anyone who claimed to have certain knowledge of something. His method, known as 'Socratic dialogue' or 'dialectic', lies behind the current practice in philosophy and other disciplines of continual critical reflection.

SOCRATES (470–399BC)

Socrates was an itinerant philosopher who wandered around his home city of Athens teaching philosophy through discourse and oratory. He served as a soldier in the Peloponnesian War (431–404BC), then became embroiled in the political turmoil which followed, before turning to stonemasonry work and raising a family. He inherited enough money from his father, a sculptor, to be sufficiently financially independent to pursue his interest in philosophy. Socrates later turned to investigating the development of moral character. He spent the latter years of his life debating with the aristocratic youths of Athens, often to the annoyance of their parents. He refused any payment for his teaching and his young followers were often fiercely loyal to him.

He was something of a maverick, and soon antagonized the citizens of Athens. He challenged their automatic belief in received ideas and wisdom, encouraging them to think critically. The citizens accused him of corrupting the minds of the young, and of not believing in the gods, and put Socrates on trial. His argumentative response to the accusations did not help his case, and when he was asked to suggest a suitable punishment for himself he recommended that he be allowed free meals in the public dining hall. This further angered the judiciary. He was offered a reprieve if he agreed to give up teaching philosophy, but he refused and was sentenced to death. He died in 399BC by drinking hemlock, surrounded by his friends and followers.

Socrates taught through debate, and left no written works. What we know of his methods and ideas comes from the writings of his contemporaries and his pupil, Plato. Socrates is considered the originator of Western philosophy, the first thinker to pursue wholly philosophical and metaphysical enquiry.

Two approaches to knowing

Just as Socrates was the teacher of Plato, so Plato was the teacher of Aristotle, placing three of the greatest thinkers in a direct line of intellectual descent. This wonderful accident of history determined the direction of Western thought for two millennia.

'The safest general characterization of the European philosophical tradition is that it consists of a series of footnotes to Plato.'

Alfred North Whitehead, *Process and Reality* (1929)

PUTTING TRUST IN REASON

Plato took up the issue of what we can know and how we discover it, and pursued it along the rationalist lines set out by Socrates.

It follows from Plato's theory of Forms that if what we perceive as the real world is but a shadow of the perfection it mimics, we cannot attain true knowledge through our senses. If we can't trust our senses to reveal truth, what can we trust? The answer Plato gives is 'reason'.

In *Meno*, Plato presents a dialogue between Socrates and Meno, a wealthy young general who has just arrived in the city with a large retinue of slaves. Socrates and Meno are debating how to define virtue and whether it can be taught. The dialogue contains Meno's paradox. Meno, confused by what Socrates is saying, asks:

'How can you look for something when you don't know what it is? Even if you find the thing, how will you know that what you have found is the thing you didn't know?'

Socrates restates this as:

'[A] man cannot search either for what he knows or for what he does not know. He cannot search for what he knows – since he knows it, there is no need to search – nor for what he does not know, for he does not know what to look for.'

Socrates tries to demonstrate to Meno that knowledge is *a priori* – pre-existing. The soul is immortal and has been exposed to knowledge before it inhabits the body that, with some prompting, it remembers during life. Socrates attempts to demonstrate this using one of Meno's slaves. The slave does not at first know a geometrical formula, but by questioning him Socrates eventually gets the boy to state the formula. Socrates claims that as he has taught the boy nothing, this is proof that the boy is remembering *a priori* knowledge.

A PRIORI AND A POSTERIORI

A priori *knowledge comes from reason alone and not from experience. Mathematical equations, for example, are examples of* a priori *knowledge, as they don't require any real-world evidence to be considered true. A priori knowledge is non-empirical.*

A posteriori *knowledge – for example, the proposition that your feet are cold or it is raining outside – is the result of experience. A posteriori knowledge is empirical.*

The final outcome of the dialogue is that knowledge is 'justified true belief'. This definition was widely accepted until 1963, when the American professor of philosophy Edmund Gettier (born 1927) pointed out that sometimes a justified true belief would not count as knowledge. This can happen when a person has a justified belief that happens to be true only by chance. For instance, a woman in love with a man with ginger hair believes she will marry him and therefore believes her future husband will have ginger hair. But she splits up with this man and marries someone else who also, by chance, has ginger hair. Her belief was justified, and it turned out to be true, but it was not knowledge.

RATIONALISM

Rationalists believe that knowledge can be discovered purely by the application of reason. They hold that knowledge does not need to be, and cannot reliably be, grounded in our experience of the world around us.

Plato presented his philosophical ideas through a series of dialogues in which Socrates debates with others, so stepping through the arguments that lead to his conclusions.

HOW ARE WE TO KNOW PHILOSOPHY?

There are different ways of presenting philosophical ideas. Some of the most important have been:

Socratic debate or *Platonic dialogue: these present two different points of view and explore them through a dramatized dialogue or dialectic. The preferred point of view can be given the more persuasive arguments and defeat the opposing view or both can be given with equal conviction, leading the listener to consider and decide the merits of the case. As a method of teaching, the point is to develop the student's skill rather than win him or her over to a particular point of view.*

Logical syllogisms, as used by Aristotle: beginning from one statement, logic is used to demonstrate that other propositions necessarily follow from it.

Aphorisms, as presented by Marcus Aurelius in his Meditations (AD170–180): *these are concise, memorable expressions of thought. No argument is presented; the aphorism stands or falls on its own perceived merits.*

Thesis/antithesis, as presented by Thomas Aquinas: Aquinas first states the question, then presents the antithesis with its supporting arguments. He follows this by stating the thesis (the preferred answer) with its supporting arguments and finally refuting the arguments in favour of the antithesis with strong counter-arguments. Hegel added 'synthesis' as a new position which results from comparing a thesis and antithesis and moving on to new knowledge.

Propositions, as presented by Ludwig Wittgenstein (1889–1951): a series of statements presented in such a way that the logical progression from first to last forms a compelling argument.

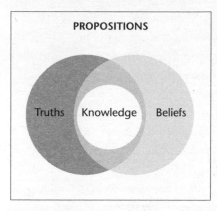

PROPOSITIONS

Truths   Knowledge   Beliefs

The area of overlap between the set of true things and the set of beliefs includes, but is not limited to, knowledge.

CHAMPION OF THE SENSES

The star pupil of Plato's Academy must have been Aristotle. He took issue with the theory of Forms and came out on the side of empirical evidence, championing what we can learn about the world through our senses. The basis of the scientific method is in Aristotelian empiricism. Aristotle taught that a thorough and methodical investigation of the world, including qualitative comparisons and assessments, can yield knowledge about phenomena. These phenomena, according to Aristotle, represent true reality, and not some shadowy version of a reality we can never truly apprehend.

PLATO (*c.*427–347BC)
Plato was born into a noble family, probably in Athens. He had two brothers and a sister, but we know little else of his early life. He was a pupil of Socrates, and in his own

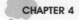

*writings he presented his philosophical ideas in the form
of dialogues between Socrates and others. It's thought that
Plato may have travelled in Italy, Sicily, Egypt and Cyrene
(Libya), and returned to Athens at the age of 40. There he
set up the first known organized school or college in the
Western world, called the Academy. It continued as an
educational establishment until it was destroyed during the
sacking of Athens by the Roman general Sulla in 86BC. One
of Plato's pupils at the Academy was Aristotle.*

*Plato often said that his purest philosophy was never
written down and he shared it only orally with close and
trusted friends and colleagues. He said the written word
was not an appropriate medium for important and difficult
material as it could not be explained or defended in the
author's absence.*

*Plato left important, influential writing about meta-
physics (the nature of reality) and epistemology (what we
can know of it), politics and ethics.*

EMPIRICISM

*Empiricism is the belief that empirical reality is accessible
to the physical senses and can be measured, observed and
known through direct interaction with the world.*

NO MORE THIS THAN THAT

The Greek philosopher Sextus Empiricus (*c.*AD160–210), left
eleven volumes of philosophy in which he set out the doctrine of
the Pyrrhonian Sceptics. These books are the only source on the
Sceptics, and we know little of Empiricus himself. The Sceptics

were a group founded around the 3rd century BC by Pyrrho (360–270BC), a philosopher who, like Socrates, wrote nothing himself. The central claim of the Sceptics is that we can't assert any proposition with more certainty or justification than we can assert its opposite. Pyrrho's philosophy is summed up in the saying 'No more this than that'. Therefore, we can be no more certain that, say, time runs relentlessly forwards than that it does not.

How does Pyrrho's philosophy work? The same object can look very different when viewed from a distance and up close, but there is no good reason to suppose the closer view is more truthful than the distant view. A vast forest, for example, can only be seen from a distance; when viewed close up, its vastness cannot be determined beyond the few trees we can see. The gap between reality and appearance cannot be closed, because what we 'know' of reality we learn through our fallible bodily senses. It is not possible to say with certainty that one thing is more likely to be true than another.

The intention of scepticism is to bring a comforting and calming disengagement from frantic questioning. But it can as readily lead to anxiety or apathy as, if no knowledge is secure, what's the point of pursuing it? Empiricus, however, says that the ultimate aims of scepticism are that it should lead to tranquillity and peace of mind.

Suppose we decide that some things are definitely good (for example, health and a loving family) and others are bad (say, poverty and friendlessness):

- We will be resentful if bad things come to us and good things do not. But if we benefit from the good things, we will be anxious about losing them.
- The sceptic, however, does not make a judgement about what is good or bad, right or wrong, and so on. Instead, he or she does not hanker after or avoid

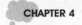
anything with great passion, but remains indifferent
to changing fortune, and so lives a tranquil life.

Of course, it is hard to live like this. Critics of scepticism point out that the claim is self-defeating. If we really can't assert one proposition over its opposite, the same is true of the sceptical claim itself – we can't say we should live like this with any more certainty than we can say that we should not live like this.

KNOWLEDGE THROUGH FAITH

With the coming of Christianity, a new conduit for knowledge appeared in the form of an omniscient God. St Augustine saw both philosophy and religion as quests for truth, though religion signified the seeking of truth of a higher order. At the heart of his philosophy was the belief that wisdom can ultimately be attained only through faith. Although some truths could be reached through reason alone, St Augustine felt that faith was

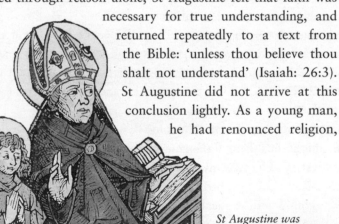

necessary for true understanding, and returned repeatedly to a text from the Bible: 'unless thou believe thou shalt not understand' (Isaiah: 26:3). St Augustine did not arrive at this conclusion lightly. As a young man, he had renounced religion,

St Augustine was born in Hippo Regius (present-day Algeria). He lived a famously intemperate life before his conversion in 389.

but after converting in his early thirties he set about showing that reason could prove the tenets of faith.

The scientific revolution

Until the 16th century, the Western world lived in the shadow of the classical period. Then, at some time around 1550 during the Renaissance in art and the humanities, a clutch of scientific advances led to a reassessment of mankind's place in the universe. It is impossible to overstate the impact of this change. In place of superstition, reverence for the authority of the ancients and blind faith, a spirit of enquiry, investigation and challenge led people to pursue truth through scientific means. The scientific writings of Aristotle, as well as those of the Greco-Roman astronomer Ptolemy (AD90–168) and the medieval scholars who had drawn on classical works, were at last called into question. The Aristotelian concept of four elements (earth, fire, air and water) making up all matter, and Ptolemy's model of the universe that placed the Earth at its centre are just two of the traditional beliefs that finally came to be challenged. Aristotle would doubtless have been amused that his preferred method of empirical investigation had dethroned his own accounts of the physical world.

Progress was neither smooth nor easy. The Church had at its heart the belief that the world is unchanging and eternal, that man is at the centre of the universe, and that the ways of God are a mystery not to be investigated. The suggestion that the Earth might not be at the centre of the universe, where Ptolemy had put it, was considered heretical by some religious authorities. Although, in 1616, the Inquisition forced the Italian astronomer Galileo Galilei (1564–1642) to recant his belief in the Copernican theory that the Earth moves around the Sun, it could not stem the tide forever. Eventually, with the weight of scientific evidence steadily building up, the stranglehold of religious dogma weakened. For the first time some scientists went so far as to doubt the existence of God and put reason above faith in the hierarchy of tools for finding out about the world.

'How could the Earth hang suspended in the air were it not upheld by God's hand? By what means could it maintain itself unmoved, while the heavens above are in constant rapid motion, did not its Divine Maker fix and establish it?'
John Calvin, *Commentary on Psalms* (1557)

THE EARTH MOVED FOR COPERNICUS

The Polish mathematician and astronomer Nikolaj Kopernik, better known as Nicolaus Copernicus (1473–1543), developed the heliocentric model of the solar system which put the Sun at the centre with the planets revolving around it. Anxious about the impact of his ideas, he did not release his treatise On the Revolution of the Celestial Spheres *for publication until just before his death in 1543.*

The Polish astronomer Copernicus proposed that the Sun is at the centre of the solar system and the Earth, along with the other planets, moves around it.

Although his ideas were known during his lifetime and attracted criticism, it took a while for them to really hit home. The Vatican added the treatise to its list of prohibited books in 1616, 73 years after Copernicus' death, even though the list had been started in 1559. The German religious reformer Philipp Melanchthon (1497–1560) said the model should be repressed by law on the grounds that 'the evidence of the senses, the thousand-year consensus of men of science, and the authority of the Bible' contradicted Copernicus.

The impact on philosophy was profound. The scientific revolution called into question the very nature of knowledge and certainty. Beliefs that had been held for nearly two thousand years slowly became untenable. What guarantee was there that those which replaced them were ultimately any more secure?

'What do I know?'

The French Renaissance writer Michel de Montaigne realized that the scientific revolution left no place for certainty. It appeared that reason is not a universal standard, nor are our senses reliable witnesses, so a degree of general scepticism seemed the most appropriate approach. Sometimes Montaigne's scepticism seems to have left him rudderless, denied all hope of certainty or direction. 'What do I know?' he asked in his essay 'An Apology for Raymond Sebond' – it was to become a refrain throughout his work. He used the case of Martin Guerre as an example. The real Martin Guerre went off to war; two years later an imposter returned home, claiming to be him. The man knew things only the real Guerre could have known and fooled even Guerre's wife. Montaigne argued that if a woman can't be certain who her husband is, what can anyone be sure of?

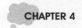

MICHEL DE MONTAIGNE (1533–92)

Michel de Montaigne was born into a wealthy French family. He had an unusual childhood, overseen by his humanist father, which involved speaking only Latin at home, three years in the care of a peasant family, and extensive exposure to music. After studying law, he worked for 11 years in regional and national courts. On his father's death in 1568, he returned to the family chateau and devoted the rest of his life to thinking and writing.

Montaigne wrote three volumes of essays reflecting on how humans relate to one another and the world. An exceptionally eloquent humanist, he applied his great erudition to a wide range of topics, and his personality shines through his writing.

Montaigne's works were not always consistent, which he would probably have regarded as a virtue. He was engaged in a sort of dialogue with himself, which continued throughout his life.

Elsewhere, Montaigne's scepticism was liberating, as Empiricus said it should be. Being freed from false certainties gives the individual more autonomy. Montaigne saw new scientific discoveries and theories contributing to an endless process of discovery – not as something that should be accepted immediately as unchallenged truth, but as steps towards what might or might not be accurate. He believed that knowledge could as easily stifle enquiry as promote it, if it were accepted uncritically. It was most important, he considered, to keep challenging and reviewing our opinions, continuing with critical enquiry, and conducting an ongoing reappraisal of the way we live.

Despite his scepticism, Montaigne was a practising Catholic. He saw no contradiction in this; on the contrary, he claimed that scepticism in non-religious matters made it easier to accept religious truths, which can only be justified through faith.

Towards science

While Montaigne was first and foremost a thinker, the English philosopher Francis Bacon (1561–1626) was at the heart of the scientific revolution.

Bacon's most notable work was on developing the scientific method. He took issue with the Platonic and Aristotelian approaches to knowledge, and considered rationalism, which approached knowledge through reason and by examining the meaning of words, to be the equivalent of spinning a web from the inside of one's own head. He thought Aristotelian empiricism involved amassing data which did not in itself yield any useful ideas. Bacon insisted that better ways of collating and organizing data would help to generate inductive hypotheses which could then be tested by scientific means.

He realized that instead of trying to show that something will always happen, there is more mileage in disproving hypotheses. This seems counter-intuitive, as it suggests that science can progress most quickly by being wrong. But it

Francis Bacon initiated the scientific method, demanding a proper investigation of any hypothesis.

does makes sense. If we toss a coin a million times and it comes down heads each time, we still can't say it will always come down heads. But if it once comes down tails, we can dismiss the hypothesis that it will always come down heads. This bears a striking resemblance to the 'falsificationist' scientific methodology developed by 20th-century philosopher Karl Popper (see page 140). In his claim to have solved the problem of induction, Popper openly acknowledged his debt to Bacon.

Francis Bacon was not primarily interested in the problem of induction, however. He was more concerned with method, and in particular with finding a method to generate good inductive hypotheses from the data that scientists were gathering.

Bacon devised a new method, which he illustrated by suggesting an investigation into the nature of heat. He said we should first list all things in which heat is present, then all things in which it is absent, and finally all those that can be of varying temperature. He believed that a natural hypothesis would present itself from the list.

THE PROBLEM OF INDUCTION
The nature of induction taxed many thinkers of the scientific revolution. In essence, it is a problem of drawing conclusions from a mass of data. If you toss a coin 20 times and it comes down heads every time, it might be tempting to suppose that it is more likely to come down tails the next time, but this is not the case. The chance of heads or tails remains the same for the first throw, the 21st throw, and for the 1,001st throw. The preceding events have no impact on the future event, and we can't

infer anything from the mass of preceding throws of the coin. Simple repetition does not guarantee anything, though it can lead us to draw up a hypothesis. So, seeing that the Sun has risen in the east every day in recorded history, we might hypothesize that it will always rise in the east. But we should need something other than previous observations to convince us that this will be the case.

His list of hot things comprised:

1. The rays of the Sun, particularly in summer, and at noon.
2. The same reflected and condensed, as between mountains, or along walls, and particularly in burning mirrors.
3. Ignited meteors.
4. Burning lightning.
5. Eruptions of flames from the cavities of mountains, etc.
6. Flame of every kind.
7. Ignited solids.
8. Natural warm water baths.

Bacon concluded that movement is the source of heat, and that hot things are characterized by movement outwards and upwards. Often it is not the whole body that moves, but the particles that make up the body – so boiling water seethes in the pot and flames dance around.

Sadly, Bacon's investigations into heat might eventually have been his downfall – he is said to have died of pneumonia while experimenting with a method for freezing chicken. But it seems unlikely that his method would often generate useful hypotheses, or that there could ever be a single way of organizing data that would make hypotheses become immediately apparent. It will always take creativity and imagination to see the patterns and potential in a body of data, and to begin building theories to account for them. Even so, Bacon is credited with the invention of the scientific method and was instrumental in making science of practical benefit to mankind, using it to produce 'inventions, which shall overcome, to some extent, and subdue our needs and miseries'. Bacon is sometimes considered to be the philosophical inspiration behind the Industrial Revolution and has been credited with first saying 'knowledge is power' (though the phrase does not appear in his writings).

THINKING AND BEING

René Descartes' most famous philosophical work is *Meditations on First Philosophy* (1641), known simply as *Meditations*, in which he set out to establish the foundations of knowledge. His own work extended far beyond philosophy to encompass various aspects of physics, including optics, and mathematics; he developed the system of Cartesian coordinates used for plotting graphs by mapping points on x, y and z axes.

In his *Meditations*, Descartes began by examining his own beliefs to decide which he felt were secure. He decided that some were easier to justify than others, with some appearing certain – such as mathematical 'truths' – and others having shakier foundations or even being revealed as false on closer inspection. He decided he needed to be able to justify each proposition by grounding it in a secure belief, but this left him with the question of where he could start – what is the infallible first proposition? Instead of trying to put all his beliefs in order, showing which followed from which, he tested each by asking, what was its source? If the source was infallible, he could consider the belief secure. If the source was fallible, no knowledge based on that source could be considered reliable.

> '*If I chance to look out of the window on to men passing in the street, I do not fail to say, on seeing them, that I see men . . . and yet, what do I see from this window, other than hats and cloaks, which cover ghosts or dummies who move only by means of springs? But I judge them to be really men, and thus I understand, by the sole power of judgement that resides in my mind, what I believed I saw with my eyes.*'
>
> René Descartes, *Meditations* (1641)

Descartes recognized that many of his beliefs were based on evidence from his senses: from what he could see, hear or feel. But our senses are not entirely reliable – a straight stick appears to be bent when placed in a glass of water, for example. Descartes then proposed that at least he could be sure he was a Frenchman interested in philosophy who was sitting in his study, and so on. But then there is no clear way of distinguishing between reality and dreaming. How does he know that the life he thinks he is leading is not just part of a dream? Hallucinations can even make us believe in something that is not there at all, with our senses deceiving us entirely. All knowledge rooted in sensory perception is therefore suspect.

Turning to his own reason, Descartes tested his knowledge that 2 + 3 = 5, that a mother is older than her daughter, and that a triangle has three sides. These beliefs look secure, but could be the result of a massive deception. He imagined the possibility of a supremely powerful, but malign, demon who could manipulate his thoughts and instil these false beliefs.

There is, however, one proposition that even a supremely powerful being could not manipulate and this is that Descartes exists because he is thinking (even though what he is thinking may be false). He must exist in order to think. Hence Descartes arrived at his famous maxim *cogito ergo sum* – 'I think therefore I am'. The *cogito*, as it is known, was his one solid, infallible foundation of knowledge.

Descartes intended to begin from the *cogito* and his certain knowledge that God exists, and in this way guarantee the security of his knowledge. But later philosophers found his subsequent arguments in the *Meditations* unconvincing, and it has instead come to be viewed as the primary text on epistemological scepticism.

Reason and experience in the Age of Reason

Descartes was a scientist as well as a philosopher and was writing at the start of the scientific and philosophical revolution that came to be known as the 'Age of Reason'. Bacon and Descartes were the earliest modern philosophers in the traditions of empiricism and rationalism which we can trace back to Plato and Aristotle. It was the German philosopher Immanuel Kant who named these two strands of philosophy. Following Descartes in the rationalist camp were Baruch Spinoza and Gottfried Leibniz, while the English philosophers Thomas Hobbes (1588–1679) and John Locke built on the earlier empiricist work of Bacon.

Locke was profoundly influenced by the scientific work of his contemporaries the English mathematician Isaac Newton (see panel opposite) and the Irish chemist Robert Boyle (1627–91). Locke set out to explain human understanding in a way consistent with Newtonian mechanics, putting epistemology on a scientific footing. He spent twenty years writing his *Essay Concerning Human Understanding* (1690), which was to exert a huge influence over the development of Western philosophy during the following 100 years.

Locke investigated how the human mind collects, organizes and classifies data and makes judgements based upon it – in his own words, 'to inquire into the original, certainty and extent of human knowledge'. He rejected the rationalist philosophy of Descartes, believing that knowledge must come from experience, through the actions of the physical world on our senses.

ISAAC NEWTON (1642–1727)

The English mathematician and physicist Isaac Newton made ground-breaking discoveries in mathematics and physics which underpinned the scientific revolution. He demonstrated that the universe runs according to predictable physical and mechanical laws. Newton's statement of the law of universal gravitation, from which he was able to explain and predict the movement of the Moon and planets, was not challenged until the work of Albert Einstein in the early 20th century. Newton's methods were empirical and inductive, and he criticized Descartes' rationalist, deductive approach to knowledge.

William Blake's idealized depiction of Isaac Newton from 1795 shows him as a god-like nude focused intently on his calculations and oblivious to the natural world around him. Blake himself was deeply opposed to the Enlightenment, writing: 'Art is the Tree of Life, Science is the Tree of Death'.

Locke introduced the idea of the mind of the newborn as a *tabula rasa*, or blank slate. The infant knows nothing, has no innate knowledge, and all that he or she learns is derived from the world of experience. The direct products of stimulation of the senses are simple ideas such as 'hot', 'cold', 'round', 'hard', 'sweet', 'yellow' and so on. These we can experience directly and require no synthesis by the mind. Complex ideas are constructed in the mind from simple ideas and require some mental operation. So, recognizing a complex idea such as a dog or a table from the collection of sensory data we receive from these objects involves thought. Complex ideas need not relate to things that exist: we can conceive of a unicorn, which does not exist but is made up of two other complex ideas, 'horse' and 'horn', which do exist.

Simple ideas are divided into primary and secondary qualities of objects. Primary qualities are those that Locke considered to be inherent and essential to all objects, such as solidity, extension in space, shape, motion or rest, and number. Secondary qualities are those that are apparent because of our sensory perception of them, such as colour, scent and taste. They are not inherent in the objects, but produced in our minds when we become aware of the objects. Primary qualities can be thought of as objective (they really exist, independent of an observer) and secondary qualities as subjective (dependent on the presence of an observer to exist). In Locke's schema, there is no such thing as colour or sound without a perceiving mind. This view is shared by some modern philosophers and scientists.

NOW YOU SEE IT, NOW YOU DON'T

Bishop George Berkeley (1685–1753) is regarded as the father of philosophical idealism; this attempted to show that the materialist view of Locke and Newton is untenable.

Berkeley was not alone in seeing that Locke's causal theory of perception implied that there is a logical gap between the subject (the perceiving mind) and reality. (This gap is sometimes called 'the veil of perception'.) When we see something, it is as a result of objects in the external world having a physical, causal effect on our senses and so producing an idea in our mind. If you look at a cat, light reflected from the cat and falling on the retina of your eye causes a signal to travel along neural pathways from the retina to the brain with the result that you 'see' a cat. The image of the cat is constructed in your brain and is no guarantee of the real existence of the cat, or that it 'really' looks the way you see it. (You could dream of a cat, or see one in a hallucination, without any real cat being present.)

SPOTLIGHT ON PHILOSOPHERS

Does a tree falling over in the forest make a sound if there is no one to hear it?

Locke: *No. It produces vibrations in the air, but sound is a secondary quality that exists only in the mind of the observer.*

Berkeley: *No. And there wasn't a tree in the first place.*

'*The objects of sense exist only when they are perceived; the trees therefore are in the garden . . . no longer than while there is somebody by to perceive them.*'

George Berkeley, *A Treatise Concerning the Principles of Human Knowledge* (1710)

Berkeley called the perception of the cat the 'idea' of the cat. It might be that cats in reality are altogether different from how we see them – we have no way of telling. Locke had backed away from this bold conclusion by distinguishing between primary qualities that really exist in an object and secondary qualities that exist only in the mind of the beholder. Berkeley saw no such distinction, so left reality without a leg to stand on.

Following this line of argument, if something is not an idea in someone's mind, it doesn't exist. If you don't see the cat, who is to say that it's there? In fact, if you don't see it, it isn't there. This is problematic, as our general belief is that things continue to exist even when we are not looking at them. If you go out of the bathroom and close the door (leaving no one else inside), do the contents of the bathroom cease to exist? Do they wink in and out of existence as you open and close the door? Berkeley had an answer to this: our perceptions are produced for us by God, and as God is all-seeing, things continue to be perceived by Him even when we are not looking. God keeps the bathroom in existence when you are no longer in it.

SCIENTIFIC ESSENTIALISM

The American philosophers Saul Kripke (born 1940) and Hilary Putnam (1926–2016) proposed a modern scheme comparable with Locke's view of essential properties. This states that all objects have essential properties that they necessarily possess if they are to be identified as a specific type of object. For example, all tigers must possess tiger DNA. Other properties, such as having striped fur and four legs, are not essential – a tiger would remain a tiger if it were an albino with no stripes or had lost a leg. The essential properties are necessary but not sufficient *to define the object in its class – so a tiger steak has tiger DNA, but is not in itself a tiger.*

PERCEPTION IS ALL, GOD IS NIL
The Scottish philosopher David Hume followed in the footsteps of Locke, claiming that only knowledge that can be gained through

our senses is valid and anything else is simply invention and must be rejected. As a consequence, he had to deny the existence of God, the self, all causation and even the validity of inductive knowledge (that derived through reasoning). Hume's scepticism was reductive in the extreme.

Observing that we can never experience our own self, only a chain of experiences, he concluded that the self is an illusion. 'I am nothing but a bundle of perceptions,' he wrote, meaning that human identity is only the sum of a stream of sense-experiences. Similarly, we don't experience or perceive the mechanism by which one event necessarily follows another (causation), we only experience the sequence of events. As we have no means of experiencing causation, Hume rejected it as illusory.

On the one hand, this seems fair: we see that one event is regularly followed by another, but this is not evidence that one causes the other. We have simply interpreted one as cause and the other as effect. It is easy to infer causation incorrectly: in the summer, sales of barbecues increase and more people go to the beach, but one does not cause the other. There is a different cause (improving weather) behind both trends. On the other hand, Hume's view doesn't allow what we would consider to be obvious and genuine causation to be acknowledged. Therefore, if you throw a stone at a window, and the window breaks, you can't, according to Hume, infer that the impact of the stone on the window causes the window to break.

QUANTUM THEORY AND OBSERVATION
In quantum physics, the role of the observer in the existence of phenomena seems to find scientific confirmation. The famous double-slit experiment and its variants examine

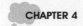

the wave/particle properties of light (and, in later versions, of electrons and even molecules). The outcome of the experiment is altered by introducing equipment to observe what is happening – in some cases, the behaviour of a particle/wave is apparently even altered retrospectively. The philosophical impact of these findings is far-reaching and implies that it is impossible to know anything if what is true is determined by the observing of it.

Hume's intention was to rid science of all falsehoods ('inventions' not based in experience) and establish a new science of human nature. In his *Treatise on Human Nature* (1739–40), he set out to find general principles or rules in psychology that would allow him to produce a mechanized view of understanding comparable to Newton's mechanized view of the physical universe. His categorization of impressions and ideas, however, owed much to Descartes, whose work he rejected. This meant that Hume failed in his goal of creating a replacement science, but succeeded in his first ambition of removing 'falsehoods'. His critique of inductive reasoning was devastating and coloured philosophy for the next two centuries.

Inductive reasoning is at the heart of all scientific endeavour: we infer scientific laws by looking at the world and searching for explanations that account for what we can see happening. Hume says that this is not a valid way to proceed, and we are not justified in assuming there are not instances we haven't observed which would disprove the 'rule'. The best response to the problem of induction comes from Karl Popper who pointed out that we can draw inferences from negative discoveries (falsification of hypotheses). So, if we see 100 brown lions and one grey lion, we can infer that not all lions are brown.

In Erwin Schrödinger's thought experiment, devised in 1935, the condition of a cat – dead or alive – is not fixed in a single state until an observer looks at it. At that point, quantum possibilities collapse and the cat ceases to be both dead and alive at the same time, and becomes either dead or alive, a proposition which Schrödinger thought ridiculous.

FROM EMPIRICISM TO POSITIVISM

Much later, the Austrian philosopher of science Ernst Mach (1838–1916) took an empiricist view that recalls Hume's extreme scepticism. He declared that:

> 'We know only one source which directly reveals scientific facts – our senses.'

No metaphysical contemplation carried any validity. In Mach's view, science should be reconstructed as an account of the facts that can be extracted from our sensory experience of the world. Anything that strays outside the description of sensory experience is stepping beyond the evidence available to us, so cannot be justified. The laws of nature that we seem to discover are, he said, simply the product of our minds wishing to impose order on our surroundings. In different cultures, places and times, different sets of explanations have been deemed suitable.

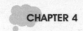

'According to our conception, natural laws are a product
of our psychological need to feel at home with nature;
all concepts transcending sensation are to be justified
as helping us to understand, control and predict our
environment, and different conceptual systems may be used
to this end in different cultures and at different times with
equal propriety.'

Ernst Mach

If the laws of nature are not laws at all, there is no way in which
they can really be 'proved' as there is no objective truth behind
them. The validity of any law of science can be measured only
insofar as it helpfully explains and structures the world for us, so
that we feel content and secure and are best able to control and
predict our environment. This leads to a pragmatic approach to
scientific theorizing. If there is more than one possible way of
explaining something, but none has the benefit of absolute truth,
how are we to choose between them? Mach suggests applying
principles of simplicity, consistency and depth. Although there
might be no absolute value in simplicity (see panel below), it
has often been thought a useful measure in choosing between
scientific theories. Consistency means there should not be
contradictions in the scheme, and depth means that it should
have great explanatory force.

OCCAM'S RAZOR

*The principle known as Occam's razor has been stated in
different forms by several philosophers. The central idea is*

that if there are two possible explanations, equally attractive in other regards, the simpler is to be preferred. In other words, the more assumptions you have to make, the more unlikely the explanation. In medicine, for example, Occam's razor is used to instruct students who are advised to test the simplest diagnosis first: 'When you hear hoof beats, think horses, not zebras.'

There is a problem with Mach's view of science. Anything we can't actually observe is, to all intents and purposes, non-existent. This includes atoms, black holes, the early geological history of the planet, tectonic plates, magnetism, gravity, time and space. Mach even said that to afford such things any material status was to invoke 'the sham ideas of the old metaphysics'. The American Willard Quine (1908–2000) made a similar point when he said that the posits of theoretical physics have no better epistemological basis than Homer's gods.

Mach's determination to rely wholly on sense-data means that he seems either to deny the existence of things we can't perceive, or deny that we can ever have knowledge of those things. In the second case, he would be aligning himself with Kant and his view of the unknowable 'noumenal world', as he called it.

Mediating between reason and experience

The divide between the empiricists on the one hand and the rationalists on the other had brought philosophy to something of an impasse in the 18th century. Over the following 200 years, there would be attempts to bridge the gap or reject both approaches in favour of an attempt at something new.

CONSTRUCTING KNOWLEDGE

Immanuel Kant tried to solve the problem by bridging the gap, showing that both approaches had some merit. In his *Critique of Pure Reason* (1781), he set out to explain how we can make objective judgements about reality. Then, in his *Critique of Practical Reason* (1788), he tried to justify ethical judgements by applying reason.

Kant began his task of reconciling reason and experience by asking, 'What are the necessary preconditions for having any experience at all?' He then suggested that we can only make sense of our experiences – the data gathered by our senses – if we have structures for interpreting them. The new, untutored mind of the newborn is not entirely a *tabula rasa*, as Locke said it was, because if the infant did not have ways of making sense of what it sees and hears, it could never construct any knowledge.

Kant argued that the mind imposes structures on incoming data. He proposed 12 fundamental judgements, or Categories: substance, cause/effect, reciprocity, necessity, possibility, existence, totality, unity, plurality, limitation, reality and negation. These Categories must be applied within the structures of space and time, which he called 'forms of intuition'. By applying Categories, with reference to the place and time where the data was received, the mind can make sense of the world. Kant was so proud of this idea that he referred to it as his 'Copernican revolution', believing that it overturned the previous world-order and finally explained how the mind generates knowledge by imposing principles on experience.

But there was a problem with Kant's approach. If the human mind could only apply structures to the data gathered by the senses, that left the reason under-employed and the realm of metaphysics untouched. The rationalists (such as Descartes) constructed knowledge purely from within the mind, and could deal with abstract concepts such as justice, beauty, the self and virtue. Kant's construction of knowledge required sense-data as the starting point for everything, so had no space for anything that doesn't begin with experience. Our knowledge can only be a systematization of experience – it can't extend to the reality beyond what we perceive, the noumenal world (see panel below).

THE NOUMENAL AND PHENOMENAL WORLDS

According to Kant, the world we experience is the phenomenal world: it is in this that we see landscapes, hear birds sing, eat food and drink wine. Our minds make sense of the data our brains receive through these experiences. What lies beyond these instances of reality is the noumenal world, 'the thing-in-itself' ('das Ding an sich'), which is not accessible to human knowledge. If we viewed everything through a distorting glass for our whole lives, we would see everything differently but be unaware that our perception was distorted. Similarly, we can't know how the perceived world (the phenomenal world) relates to the real state of the world (the noumenal world).

THE PATH TO TRUTH

Although Kant considered the gap between the noumenal and the phenomenal worlds (the real and perceived) to be unavoidable, Hegel found it unacceptable and wanted to close it. He believed there was an ultimate truth, and it was accessible to human understanding. The path to discovery lay in a process called 'dialectic', which takes place over the whole, slowly unfolding history of human thought. Hegelian dialectic begins with a notion, or thesis, that is deemed to be true. If we reflect on this thesis, we discover that there is another possible point of view that contradicts it. This is called the 'antithesis'. Comparison and consideration of these opposing points of view often reveals a third way that might be something of a compromise, or a middle path. This is called the 'synthesis'. The synthesis becomes the new thesis and then a new antithesis emerges to contradict it, and so a new synthesis must be found, and so on. Through a process of iteration, we creep closer to truth.

But it is not a truth in the sense that one proposition is true and another is not. For Hegel, truth was not propositional; instead, it was conceptual, and to do with completeness. The progression towards truth is really a progression towards a universal mind or spirit. In Hegel's scheme, a scientific theory that has been shown to be wrong or inadequate is merely incomplete. The Newtonian laws of gravitation were accepted as wholly correct for many centuries, but Einstein showed that they don't apply to very small bodies (such as atoms) and perhaps not to bodies larger than galaxies. This didn't make the law of gravitation wrong – it just meant it was limited, an incomplete understanding of the absolute truth. Attaining absolute truth means overcoming all limitations. It ends with a grand metaphysical concept of a universal mind.

Arthur Schopenhauer was a contemporary of Hegel. Although he disliked Hegel, Schopenhauer also took as his starting point the unknowability of things-in-themselves, the 'real' reality behind the phenomenal world as described by Kant. But Schopenhauer posited a means by which we *can* know things-in-themselves. He argued that, 'We ourselves are among those entities we want to know, so we too are a thing-in-itself.' He meant that the subjective 'I' is only revealed to us in the world of phenomena, so it can't constitute our real essence (the 'thing-in-itself'). Our real essence is will, the universal striving force manifest, trapped, in each individual being by its insatiable desire to reveal itself in the world of appearances. Recognizing the will lets us know the 'thing-in-itself' that is the 'I'.

'The significance of that "absolute" commandment,
"know thyself", whether we look at it in itself or under
the historical circumstance of its first utterance – is
not to promote mere self-knowledge in respect of the
particular capacities . . . of the single self. The knowledge
it commands means that of man's genuine reality – of what
is essentially and ultimately true and real – of spirit as the
true and essential being.'

George Hegel

THE RISE OF PHENOMENALISM

The German mathematician and philosopher Edmund Husserl
saw science not as an empirical enterprise but as principally
rational. Like Descartes, he thought philosophy must begin
with the self-evidence of the individual's subjectivity. Science, in
Husserl's view, is an exploration of perception, belief, judgement
and other mental processes rather than of the world 'out there'.
This position – that we can only deal with the sense-impressions
made on us by phenomena, and cannot deal directly with whatever
'reality' causes those impressions – is called *phenomenalism*. It
is central to existentialism and, after Husserl, was explored by
Heidegger, Merleau-Ponty and Sartre.

PHENOMENALISM

*Phenomenalism is essentially subjective: it says that all we
have to work with is how we experience the world through
our senses rather than what the world really is.*

*There are different levels of phenomenalism. Kant can
be called an epistemological phenomenalist, as he believed*

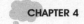

> *that all we can know is the act of experiencing. George Berkeley can be called an ontological phenomenalist, as he believed that all that exists is the act of experiencing.*

Husserl began with the concept of 'intentionality', which he took from German psychologist Franz Brentano (1838–1917). According to Brentano, all mental acts are directed towards an object. If we think of the city of Paris, the thought is directed towards the object, Paris. If we rage against injustice, our anger is directed towards injustice (the object can be abstract in nature). If we fear ghosts, the fear is directed towards ghosts (the object need not exist in reality – the fear exists whether or not ghosts exist). Husserl suggested that the intentionality of the mind entails that the conscious state (thought, rage, fear) can't be separated from its object (Paris, injustice, ghosts). They exist together, as two aspects of one phenomenon, the intentional act.

So, Husserl saw consciousness as 'directedness towards an object' (whether or not there is a physical external object). The aim of philosophy, he believed, is to understand how this directedness manifests itself. He considered this a non-empirical version of science: one that investigates only the subjective elements of the mental processes of experience.

Husserl's investigation didn't pay any heed to what, if anything, 'out there' lies behind the mental act. He was interested only in what he could consider certainties, and they lay within the conscious mind and the acts of consciousness. Like Descartes, Husserl realized he could not say anything certain about the world 'out there', outside the mind. By his own definition, consciousness is identified with the intentional act, but it is not the act, it is observing the act. The self (or consciousness) can't be the object of an intentional act because it can't be both observed and observer. Husserl was led to conclude that the subject of experience (the self) is transcendental – inhabiting some other realm. This was a return to Descartes' dualist position in which the self and the external world (and by extension, the mind and the body) occupy distinct realms.

The French philosopher Maurice Merleau-Ponty (1908–61) was greatly influenced by Husserl and also adopted a phenomenological approach, focusing on the embodied experience without reference to the objective reality of the world experienced.

Merleau-Ponty found empiricism and rationalism unsatisfactory, partly because they failed to answer Meno's paradox – that you can't look for something you don't know, because you won't recognize it if you find it.

Empiricists look at the world as something separate from the mind – the conscious mind is the subject and the world is the object. We experience the world in a rich, multi-layered way, and always in a complex context. But to make sense of it, we try to order it, breaking this continuum of experience into discrete chunks. We can't know whether the way we put these chunks together in our minds is an accurate representation of the reality (assuming there is an objectively real world). This means that the external world remains unknowable, and Meno's paradox stands. Rationalism (which Merleau-Ponty calls intellectualism) also falls foul of Meno's paradox: if knowledge exists *a priori*, then why do we need to search for it?

Merleau-Ponty put perception at the core of his scheme and saw it as experienced through the 'lived body'. He rejected rationalism because it gives no importance to perception in the process of acquiring knowledge and is not concerned with the body and the reality of our existence as embodied beings. He also rejected empiricism because it breaks down sense-perceptions in an atomistic way that does not relate to reality as we experience it. Merleau-Ponty believed that the subject (consciousness) is not something which exists only in the mind, but is experienced in and through the whole body. He rejected Descartes' view of the body as a physiological mechanism inhabited by a separate and 'other' spirit and instead saw body and mind as an integrated mechanism. The mind is not simply an inhabitant and the act of perception is not just the impact of sense-data on sensory organs, but something that involves the intellect.

We derive meaning from our experiences through the way we perceive them in relation to our bodies – hot or cold, big or small, near or far. Our experience of spatial location depends on how our own bodies occupy space and a specific location. Our experience of time is dictated by our inability to inhabit any moment but the present, so defining our sense of the past and future.

Describing experience as a subject-object dialogue, Merleau-Ponty reminded us that each experience is perceived with everything that surrounds it in space and everything that has preceded it in time. He broke out of the mind/world dualism and put the body in a third state between them. He also resolved Meno's paradox: how do we know we have found what we are looking for if we don't yet know what it is? Because the embodied experience gives it meaning. At first, our perceptions are fuzzy and ambiguous, but as we become more bodily engaged with the world, things become more defined and certain.

'Empiricism cannot see that we need to know what we are looking for, otherwise we would not be looking for it, and intellectualism fails to see that we need to be ignorant of what we are looking for, or equally again we should not be searching.'

Maurice Merleau-Ponty,
The Phenomenology of Perception (1945)

Looking sideways at reality

Empiricism flourished in the 20th century, perhaps encouraged or supported by rapid advances in science and the increasing interest that philosophers took in the basis of scientific knowledge. The British philosopher Alfred Ayer (1910–89), better known as A. J. Ayer, was an empiricist in the tradition of Hume. He developed a robust form of empiricism which he called 'linguistic phenomenalism'. Generally, phenomenalism considers objects in the material world to be constructions in the mind made from sense-data. In Ayer's version, statements about material objects are only statements about the sense-data we receive, as the objects are not observable or knowable.

Ayer maintained that any statement about material objects can be reduced to statements about sense-data. Therefore, if we see a tree in a garden, all we can really say is that if we go to a place that is known as the garden we will experience sense-data about (that is, see) something which exhibits 'tree-ness'. And the reason we will see something which exhibits tree-ness is because that is what happens if you go into that garden (not necessarily because there is a tree, or anything else which exhibits tree-ness). Although Ayer was attempting to be more rigorous in what we can be certain about, he ended up with something rather vague and uncertain.

LOGICAL POSITIVISM

Ayer is perhaps best remembered for the doctrine of logical positivism, which holds that scientific knowledge is the only kind of factual knowledge and rejects all metaphysical doctrines as meaningless. According to logical positivists, 'true' statements fall into two categories: they are either 'tautologies', which are the truths of mathematics and logic, or they are the verifiable empirical claims of science. Any other type of statements, including questions about metaphysics or religion, are not simply untrue, they are meaningless because they're not genuine statements. The logical positivists depended on the principle of verificationism: this means the validity of a statement rests on its ability either to be verified from experience or by virtue of its being 'analytic' (demonstrable by logic starting from a statement which is accepted as true). Beginning before the outbreak of World War II, logical positivism arose from the Vienna Circle and Berlin Circle, groups of philosophers sharing ideas and based in these two major European cities.

VERIFYING AND FALSIFYING

The philosopher Karl Popper responded to verificationism with a method he called 'falsificationism', by which he claimed to have solved Hume's problem of induction. Hume believed that by examining collected data we can see patterns that lead us to theories or to extracting rules. The difficulty is that we can never examine all possible examples. For example, we might decide on the basis of observation that all foxes are red or all swans are white. But we haven't seen every fox and every swan; people believed all swans were white until black swans were seen. There's nothing to say that we won't one day find a green fox. These conclusions drawn from observation (induced) are not robust, as a single counter-example can overturn them.

Popper pointed out that it's easier to disprove a theory than to verify it. He said a generalization is not valid as a conclusion drawn from evidence, but has the logical status of a conjecture. It can be tested by observations that will either refute it (if we see a green fox, for instance) or it waits to be tested by further observations. The generalization that all foxes are red becomes a conclusion only if we have seen all foxes that have ever existed or will ever exist.

The mark of a scientific theory is that it can be falsified. Popper rejected psychoanalysis as a science on the grounds that its theories cannot be falsified. He saw the accumulation of scientific knowledge over time as a result of repeated falsification. As one theory after another is shown to be wrong, the stock of remaining theories (or replacement theories) is slowly whittled away, leaving those that are correct.

Willard Quine was an empiricist *par excellence*. He maintained that science is 'the final arbiter of truth' and only science can tell us about the world. Even so, our knowledge of the world is limited by our reception and interpretation of sense-data. In *Two Dogmas of Empiricism* (1951), Quine took a stand against established positivist positions. First he attacked Kant's distinction between analytic propositions, which are by definition true (such as 'all corpses are dead'), and synthetic propositions, which are true or false according to circumstance (that it is raining, for example). Then Quine rejected the claim that a statement about the material world can be reduced to statements about sense-data.

ANALYTIC AND SYNTHETIC STATEMENTS
Analytic statements are true by definition – such as, 'all bachelors are unmarried'.
Synthetic statements have a specific subject and predicate – such as, 'that bachelor is 25 years old'.

Quine argued that all propositions are tied in with sensory experience and with the 'web of beliefs' in which we are embedded. We can't dissociate our experiences from the world-view we hold, so theory and experience necessarily go hand in hand. Science is essentially a pragmatic exercise that fits experience to what we can know and predicts future experience in the light of past experience. Quine accepted that ontology (the philosophical study of being) is relative to the beliefs of any particular society.

> '*For my part I . . . believe in physical objects and not in Homer's gods; and I consider it a scientific error to believe otherwise. But in point of epistemological footing, the physical objects and the gods differ only in degree and not in kind. Both sorts of entities enter our conceptions only as cultural posits.*'
>
> Willard Quine, *Two Dogmas of Empiricism* (1951)

FIGHTING BACK

The Austrian-born philosopher Paul Feyerabend (1924–94) rejected both logical positivism and Popper's falsificationism. He became famous in the 1960s and 1970s for establishing 'epistemological anarchism', which attacked the assumption that science is rooted in a rational methodology.

Feyerabend began with an idea proposed by Thomas S. Kuhn (1922–96) which states that science oscillates between periods of 'normal science' and 'revolutionary science'. According to Kuhn, normal scientific progress takes place as a 'development-by-accumulation' of accepted facts and theories, with only findings that endorse the current paradigm being given serious consideration. Then there are occasional periods of revolutionary science during which everything is up for grabs; the discovery of 'anomalies' during these periods leads to new paradigms. Feyerabend refuted Kuhn's assertion by arguing that there are always incompatible scientific theories vying for attention, and it is the competition between them that makes scientific endeavour fruitful. Even if a theory is considered adequate, he stated, it is good to suggest alternatives because the challenge forces us to examine how robust the theory really is and to test it further. Feyerabend called this method 'theoretical pluralism'. It led him towards 'relativism' and 'anti-realism'. He rejected the usual wisdom that a theory is good if it 'fits the facts' because he didn't accept that there were facts to be fitted. Feyerabend considered that all statements of fact are bound up with the beliefs and conventions that attach to the words in which they are couched. Here he draws on the 'language-game' idea of Ludwig Wittgenstein, which says that all use of language is limited by social context.

Feyerabend argued that factual statements don't reflect some independent reality but are determined by social conventions and the connotations of words, and that these in turn reflect a prevailing view of the world. He suggests that instead of comparing a theory with 'facts' we should compare competing theories with each other and choose the one that adds most to our understanding.

Feyerabend's doctrine of epistemological anarchism had it that there are no rules or methods in science that will reliably produce good results, so science is essentially anarchic. Most academics paid little regard to this extreme position, but Feyerabend enjoyed popularity among some alternative groups who resisted the dogma of science.

Paul Feyerabend alienated other philosophers with his view that no theory or factual statement in fact reflects a real state of affairs.

> 'There is only one principle that can be defended under all circumstances and in all stages of human development. It is the principle: anything goes.'
>
> Paul Feyerabend, *Against Method* (1975)

What is truth?

We have discussed at length how philosophers believe we arrive at knowledge, at what we can consider 'true', but we have said little about what truth is. The working definition of knowledge is 'a true belief', rooted in Plato's assertion that knowledge is a justified belief. By definition, to have knowledge is to be in possession of information that is true because if we 'know' something that is not true, we don't really know it; we simply believe it.

> 'To say of what is that it is not, or of what is not that it is, is false, while to say of what is that it is, and of what is not that it is not, is true.'
>
> Aristotle, *Metaphysics*

But what is 'true'? Perhaps truth corresponds to some form of reality – whether empirical reality or a realm of ideal Forms. This is the 'correspondence' theory of truth. The nature of truth is a question in metaphysics, but one that clearly lies at the heart of epistemology. Thomas Aquinas gave a succinct statement of correspondence:

> 'Truth is the conformity of the intellect to the things.'

WHAT CAN WE KNOW?

Aquinas also said that real things participate in God's creation, and God is truth. The human intellect, he believed, is able to apprehend the essence of things because of its spiritual, God-participating aspect.

There is clearly a problem with the correspondence definition of truth, as pointed out by Kant. We have to rely on our judgement to tell us whether we have accurately judged the truth of something (whether it corresponds to reality), so we are judging our own judgement. It's not a robust test.

KNOWLEDGE IS POWER (IN THE WRONG HANDS)

The French social theorist Michel Foucault (1926–84) was the first post-modernist philosopher. The relationship between power and knowledge, and how power is used to control and define knowledge runs through all of Foucault's work. He saw scientific knowledge not as a means of empowering ordinary people, but as a method of social control. During the 18th century, for example, the label of 'madness' – the opposite of 'reason' – was used to stigmatize not just the mentally ill but all kinds of socially undesirable people. These included the poor, the homeless and anyone else considered a social nuisance. Foucault considered the replacement of public executions with prison sentences to be another demonstration of power. He didn't believe prison had become the main form of punishment simply because of the humanitarian concerns of reformists, but argued that by exercising this extended and dehumanizing punishment the state could more effectively demonstrate its power in a generalized and controlled fashion.

With Freudian psychoanalysis, the focus on sexuality as an aspect of psychology provided another way of controlling people. If sexual intentions and preferences give an insight into personality, people become wary of revealing too much about themselves while simultaneously being encouraged to be more open about their sexuality. All these aspects of knowledge and identity change through time, but they don't vary along a path of linear progress. Instead, they change as those in power use them for their own ends to control the behaviour of others.

Foucault maintained that this dismal state of affairs could be countered by using philosophy to redress the power balance. We need to re-examine our ideas about how knowledge is socially constructed as a tool of manipulation and control. Once we have recognized how those in power control us, we can think of ways to prevent it.

REDEFINING TRUTH

Søren Kierkegaard divided truths into 'objective' and 'subjective'. Objective truths, such as the laws of mathematics, are confirmed by science and other statements about the external world in relation to itself, and statements about the facts of being. Subjective truths are statements about an individual's internal world, the relationship of the individual to the world – the way of being. These vary between individuals, and their truth-value is constantly changing and evolving. Subjective truth is dynamic, while objective truth is static.

Nietzsche wrote in *Beyond Good and Evil* (1886):

'The falseness of a judgement is to us not necessarily an objection to a judgement. . . . The question is to what extent it is life-advancing, life-preserving, species-preserving, perhaps even species-breeding.'

The American philosopher John Dewey (1859–1952) held that 'truth' as a measure of how well an account or model fits reality is worthless. He suggested instead that we accept as 'true' the interpretation of events which proves most useful – the one that gives us a way of living and working in the world as we find it. He called this 'warranted assertibility' – the status a proposition gains through the ongoing, self-correcting processes of enquiry. This effectively meant that 'truth' didn't have to be 'true' any more, in the common-sense definition of the word.

The American philosopher Richard Rorty (1931–2007) was influenced by Dewey. Rorty felt that the long philosophical search for foundational values, or *a priori* truths, would never 'produce noncontroversial results concerning matters of ultimate concern'. He rejected the Cartesian attempt to make philosophy a science; this, he felt, had led to hundreds of years of debate between rationalists and empiricists, idealists and materialists which had got us nowhere. The idea that the mind is a 'theatre of representations', forever dealing with a reality outside itself, was faulty. So, too, was the later attempt to replace mind in the equation with language, and the earlier model with God in place of science.

In place of what he considered to be intellectually bankrupt traditions, Rorty offered 'epistemological behaviourism'. The central premise of this is that we know what our society lets us know. What we accept has nothing to do with how well a statement mirrors the world, and everything to do with how well it fits in with what we already believe. The answer to the question of why we believe what we believe will be found in psychology, sociology or biology, but not in philosophy.

Thinkers throughout the ages – Copernicans, Marxists and modern scientists, in one of Rorty's examples – came up with sentences that redescribe reality, such as 'the Earth goes round the Sun', 'all history is the history of class struggles' and 'matter can be changed into energy'. These redescriptions were initially seen as false, then accepted as hypotheses, and finally 'became accepted, at least within certain communities of inquiry, as obviously true'. Since there are no ultimate truths, Rorty felt that truth cannot be a meaningful goal of inquiry. Philosophers should aim instead for the practical matter of 'honest justification'. Those beliefs which 'work', that help to achieve a culture's aims, are the ones that can be justified.

What can we say?

For the last 150 years or so, the slipperiness and imprecision of language itself has emerged as a major strand in philosophy. The need to express philosophical thoughts – or all thoughts – in language has led to the concern that what we can say or even think is proscribed by the language we have to use. What we understand of what other people say is distorted by our own understanding of language. In what way does language relate or correspond to any type of reality?

'When they (my elders) named some object, and accordingly moved towards something, I saw this and I grasped that the thing was called by the sound they uttered when they meant to point it out. Their intention was shown by their bodily movements, as it were the natural language of all peoples: the expression of the face, the play of the eyes. . . . Thus as I heard words repeatedly used in their proper places in various sentences, I gradually learnt to understand what objects they signified; and . . . I used them to express my own desires.'

St Augustine, *Confessions*, I. 8

Unfortunately, language is our main way of communicating with one another. Words have meaning because they have accrued that meaning over time, through use and re-use. With concrete nouns – dog, chair, umbrella, and so on – it's quite easy for us to agree on a meaning, at least at a fairly functional level. Or so it would appear. In fact, there is a lot of extra knowledge we need in order to agree: what makes a fox not a dog? How is a parasol not an umbrella? It becomes harder with abstracts and with adjectives, prepositions and other non-concrete words. Words have connotations and implications that are often dependent on the social or intellectual context in which they are used. For example, if I said to my teenage daughter 'Granddad is sick', she would know I meant he was unwell. If I said 'That jumper is sick', she would know I meant it was a great jumper. But if I said 'That video is sick', she would not know whether I meant it was a really good video, or a distasteful video with degrading or offensive content.

A philosopher such as Heidegger – who distrusted and discarded much of the established vocabulary of philosophical discourse – might coin new terms to avoid inappropriate or inconvenient accretions of meaning, but the problem is that no one else would know what those new terms meant. So the philosopher must define new terms or write in such a way that their meaning becomes apparent – emerges – from the context. There are some coinages in this book – 'dough-not', 'giraffe-ness', 'what/ever' – which illustrate this point.

THE START OF SEMIOTICS
The Swiss linguist Ferdinand de Saussure (1857–1913) is often considered to be the founder of semiotics (the study of how signs are used to create meaning). He saw

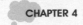
language as a system of signs; each word is a sign that can be seen as a signifier-and-signified pairing. The signifier is the spoken (or written) word, a pattern of sounds. The signified is the thing or concept that the word denotes. The pattern of sounds that relates to any particular concept is fundamentally arbitrary, so although we can trace the sound of a word such as 'cat' through different languages, there is no reason why that sound rather than any other should be linked with the concept of 'cat'.

Language can be analyzed independently of the words that make it up. It forms a system by which humans can constitute and articulate their world.

Language is essentially social; it is a shared sign system that, in order to make meaning, needs other people to be able to decode the signs. The sound and meaning (signifier and signified) are both 'deposited in the mind' by a speech event. The signifier and signified are like 'the front and back of a single sheet of paper'. Words are given meaning by virtue of the differences between them and other words, therefore 'male' and 'female' require each other in order to be meaningful.

THE 'LINGUISTIC TURN'

The interest in linguistic philosophy began with the work of German mathematician, logician and philosopher Gottlob Frege, who challenged the definition of a proposition which had been accepted since Aristotle formulated it, and recast language according to a mathematical model. If we take the sentence 'Socrates is wise', the Aristotelian (syllogistic) way of describing it is to say it has a subject, 'Socrates', and a predicate, 'is wise'. Frege separated the sentence into an argument, 'Socrates', and a function, 'is wise'. We can take Socrates out and see what kind of word needs to go in its place:

( ) *is wise*

This is like a mathematical statement in which the arguments can be replaced in a function:

$( ) + ( )$

As neither the argument nor the function means anything in isolation and the sentence only has meaning in its entirety, it is then clear that context is what bestows meaning. Frege goes further to show that there is a gap between the referent (what is being discussed) and the sense of a sentence. For example, suppose there is a film star called Fifi Ambergris and we are talking about her. I call her 'that plastic bimbo' but you call her 'that Oscar-winning beauty'; we mean different things (the sense is different), but we are referring to the same person (Fifi Ambergris).

THE COIFFURE OF THE KING OF FRANCE

The British philosopher Bertrand Russell (1872–1970) was concerned with problems of meaning and reference. He tackled the question of whether a sentence such as 'The present King of France is bald' can be said to be true, false or meaningless. This sentence is said to 'not refer', because the subject (the present King of France) does not exist. If we say it is false, this implies the contrary (that the King of France is not bald) is true. But the statement is clearly not true, either. And it is not meaningless because we can understand what it is saying.

Russell proposed that such sentences consist of separate claims, which must be separately assessed. In this case, the first proposition (that there is a present King of France) is false. Only one claim needs to be false for the whole to be rejected as false, so we can now reject this statement as false. This is the theory of 'definite descriptions'. It is useful because it means we can talk meaningfully about things that don't exist.

WITTGENSTEIN VERSUS AUGUSTINE

Frege influenced the early work of Ludwig Wittgenstein, one of the most famous philosophers of language. Wittgenstein initially published to great acclaim, then spent his later life renouncing what he had said and trying to come up with a better account. In his *Tractatus Logico-Philosophicus* (1922), Wittgenstein took issue with what he called 'the Augustinian picture of language'. Although he was only 32 years old when *Tractatus* was published, Wittgenstein claimed it answered all the questions of philosophy and there was no more to do, then promptly retired from active academic life.

Tractatus tackles the relationship between language, thought and reality. Wittgenstein followed Frege in saying that the meaning of any expression must be determined by the nature of the world – without context, everything is vague and meaningless. And he followed Bertrand Russell in saying that language and the world must be understood in terms of their constituent parts. But he went further in saying that the underlying structure of sentences must mirror the structure of the world. He said that sentences must be representations – pictures – of possible states of affairs. This is his 'picture theory' of language. Wittgenstein denied that the structure of language could be imperfect in terms of its logic. Anything that can be said, he claimed, can be said clearly. Anything that can't be said clearly must be 'passed over in silence'.

Although initially immensely pleased with *Tractatus*, Wittgenstein later had second thoughts. After going into voluntary exile for a while, he returned to Cambridge in 1929 and set about trying to revise it. For the next 20 years – until he died – he tried to clarify what he had meant and remove confusion, strongly criticizing his earlier work while all around were still praising it.

In *Philosophical Investigations* (1952), published after his death, Wittgenstein reversed his thinking, saying that meaning is not in fact dependent on reality, nor is language concerned with representing the world. Words help to elucidate meaning. Therefore, by indicating a dog it helps us to see what the concept 'dog' means. By indicating lots of different dogs, it makes the meaning a bit clearer because we can see which features of the dogs are essential to their dog-ness (being brown is not essential, but having four legs generally is, and so on).

Wittgenstein saw that language has many functions and words can be used as tools in different ways – not just to describe things but to ask questions, give orders, insult people, lie and manipulate. The meaning of a word depends on how it is being used at the time; words are defined by how they are used. His notion of a 'language-game' rests on this: that meaning is not tied to reality, but must be deduced or untangled from the context in which a word is used. The behaviour of language-users explains and defines the meanings of words.

SPEECH ACTS

Like Wittgenstein in *Philosophical Investigations*, the British philosopher of language John Austin (1911–60) was interested in how language is used for different purposes – for different kinds of 'speech-act', as he called them. In *How to Do Things with Words* (1962), Austin described three types of speech act. In the first type, words have their literal meaning, saying something about the world. For instance, 'the cat sat on the mat' tells us there was a cat and a mat and shows the relationship between them. This he called a 'locutionary act'. Sometimes, words can serve another function, such as asking a question, making a promise or giving an order – 'put the cat on the mat', for instance. This he calls an 'illocutionary act'. Finally, some utterances are an action. Saying 'I do' at a wedding gets you married; agreeing a deal on a house makes you a house-owner. These are 'perlocutionary acts'. A speech-act can serve more than one of these functions at a time. 'The cat is on the mat!' can mean 'get that cat off the precious mat immediately' and is an instruction, an illocutionary act. If someone removes the cat as a result, it has worked as a perlocutionary act. Understanding these acts, according to Austin, changes our idea of meaning in language. The first two – locutionary and illocutionary acts – depend on convention and context for us to understand what is meant. If we don't share certain rules of language use with the speaker, we will not necessarily know what they are talking about.

> *'The only absolute truth is that there are no absolute truths.'*
>
> Paul Feyerabend (1924–94)

CHAPTER 5
How should we live?

'It has been shown that to injure anyone is never just anywhere.'
Socrates, in Plato's *Republic*

'All rational creatures go out upon the sea of life with their minds made up on the common questions of right and wrong.'
John Stuart Mill, *Utilitarianism* (1861)

'That actions are at once obligatory and at the same time unenforceable is what puts them in the category of the ethical.'
David Couzens Hoy, Professor of Philosophy, University of California (2004)

The debate about how we may live a virtuous life makes up the branch of philosophy known as ethics. It was first addressed by Socrates in the 5th century BC. It encompasses questions such as how we decide which actions are moral and ethical and which are not; whether morality is universal or relative; and how free we are to act in what we perceive to be an ethical way. Some might argue that responsibility for moral action is only meaningful if people can choose how to behave, whether they have free will and the power to be self-determining in their particular circumstances.

Free will and predestination

The question of whether we are free to make choices or are treading a path already laid out for us, from which we cannot deviate, has been asked for thousands of years. While the responsibility for our destiny used to be in the hands of the gods or fate, it is now believed to be physics that controls our behaviour.

The Ancient Greeks and Romans made trips to the oracles to find out what was going to happen to them and what they should do about it. But stories such as that of Oedipus – who unwittingly killed his father and married his mother – underline the perceived impotence of humans in the face of their destiny.

Aristotle outlined the problem by describing a sea battle. There might or might not be a sea battle tomorrow, he said. When tomorrow comes, if there is a sea battle, we should be able to say that the previous day it would have been true to say that there was going to be a sea battle. Therefore, the battle looks as though it must inevitably happen and the future is entirely determined by past truths. But although Aristotle believed most things could be traced to causes, he made allowance for some accidents – for 'fresh starts' – in the sequence of events. Some of these accidents depend on ourselves, on the things we do; so it appears we do have some control over events after all.

The Stoics took a more rigorous line. They believed that what will happen in the future is predetermined (and for the best). Nevertheless, they allowed sufficient freedom of action to consider it worth telling people they should order their thoughts to accept this state of affairs. If everything was 100 per cent predetermined, a person who was not destined to accept the Stoic position could never accommodate themselves to it.

This last point highlights the biggest problem with a doctrine of strict determinism: if humans are not able to affect the course of fate, there is no point in them acting at all. What will be, will be, regardless of what we do. There is, then, no incentive to do anything difficult. It is a doctrine that can be taken as a wastrel's charter, a licence for indigence and sloth.

DETERMINISM
Determinism is the belief that everything that will happen in the future is already mapped out (determined) and can't be altered by human actions.

PREDESTINATION PARADOX
Literature often makes use of the 'predestination paradox'. The story of Oedipus is a popular example of this. Laius, king of Thebes, hears a prophecy that his son will kill him

and marry his widow. Hoping to avoid this brutal end, Laius gives orders for his baby son, Oedipus, to be left exposed on a mountain with his feet pierced in the expectation that he will die.

But Oedipus is rescued and raised by a shepherd. When he is fully grown, Oedipus hears the same prophecy and decides to leave home to avoid killing the shepherd who he believes to be his beloved father. But fate is not so easily thwarted. Oedipus meets Laius' entourage on the road. There is a fight (of course, this is Ancient Greece) and Oedipus kills his father. He then journeys on to Thebes and marries the royal widow, becoming king of Thebes. When he learns that he has, indeed, killed his father and married his mother, he tears out his own eyes.

Science fiction stories and films often use the pre-destination paradox in the form of a time loop. A character travels backwards in time to prevent a specific event and ends up causing that very event, so the trip through time itself becomes a necessary part of its own history.

BARRIERS TO FREE ACTION

There are more ways to deny a person free will than to say that everything is predetermined. There are physical constraints: a person can't operate freely if chained up or imprisoned. Some events necessarily follow others for physical reasons – so if you knock over a cup, the liquid in it will spill out (physical determinism, or causation). Humans also use psychological constraints or bullying – trying to control the actions of another by threats or coercion. Indoctrination or established beliefs can also prevent an individual from exploring alternatives or ever considering another path.

Shakespeare's Hamlet is a character paralyzed by free will. Unable to work out the best course of action, he does nothing until events overtake him.

God knows what's going on

For some people, the belief in an omniscient God seems to preclude free will. After all, if God knows what is going to happen, including whatever it is you are going to do tomorrow, how can you be free to act as you wish? But God is extra-temporal, existing outside the stream of time. His seeing things does not make them happen, any more than you seeing the Sun rise makes that happen. He observes what happens in an eternal present. This is similar to the argument put forward by the English friar William of Ockham (1288–1348), for whom necessity and possibility are defined relative to a point in time and a set of circumstances, so an event that looks only possible to us may appear as necessary to God.

DAMNED IF YOU DO, AND DAMNED IF YOU DON'T

It might seem that it doesn't much matter whether or not God knows what will happen until we consider the thorny issue of salvation. Many of the Church Fathers – the very early Christian teachers and thinkers – argued that God had given humankind free will. Along with free will comes the responsibility to choose good actions over bad actions, and culpability for the wrong choice. Without freedom, we could not be held responsible for what we did, so could not fairly be punished for sinful behaviour.

This notion of ethical responsibility was derailed by the doctrine of original sin. If we are born sinful, the dice are weighted against us. Pelagian heresy (named after the 4th-century Celtic monk and ascetic Pelagius) attempted to deal with this issue by stating that original sin did not taint human nature and people are still capable of choosing good or evil without special assistance from God. Pelagius was concerned about the poor moral standards among his fellow Christians and he tried to improve their conduct through his teachings. He held that each individual is fully responsible for every one of their sins and for following the teachings of the gospel. Sinners are criminals who have freely chosen depravity when they could have chosen to be virtuous. The virtuous are rewarded for their choice with salvation.

THE STORY OF SIR GOWTHER

The medieval verse romance Sir Gowther *tells of a young man who is the child of a demon-rapist and a mortal woman. As an infant and young child, Gowther's inherent evil is manifest. He sends numerous wet nurses to their graves and indulges in other types of demonic behaviour. When he is older he roams the land with a giant sword, terrorizing everyone, in particular the religious orders (he burns a convent of nuns to death). Then someone tells him that his perversity is the result of his parentage – he is only evil because he is half-demon. Gowther is infuriated by this explanation and decides to be truly perverse by rebelling against his devilish nature. He turns to doing good deeds.*

The question is, are his acts of charity and benevolence of any moral value, given that he does them out of a desire to be perverse and unnatural? For a virtue ethicist such as Socrates, they are not moral. For a deontological ethicist such as Kant, they are moral, because Gowther is following the rules of acceptable behaviour – not terrorizing people, not burning nuns to death, and so on. And for a consequentialist, such as Jeremy Bentham (see page 179), they are moral because people benefited from Gowther's good deeds.

St Augustine, following the Epistle of St Paul, overturned the Pelagian heresy. He argued that all humans are born into sin and that redemption is only possible through the grace of God. Adam has already condemned all mankind to damnation. Repentance and virtuous living are the only possible paths to salvation, but it is not guaranteed – we still need divine intervention to save us. His view was supported by Anselm of Canterbury (1033–1109), Thomas Aquinas, the Scottish cleric John Duns Scotus (1266–1308) and the Protestant reformer Martin Luther.

The French theologian John Calvin was strongly influenced by St Augustine, and his doctrine of election is rooted in the belief that God has already chosen those who will be saved by grace. It means that no matter how well or how badly we behave, our destiny as elect or not cannot be changed. This seems to suggest there is no incentive to act well, but those who accepted the doctrine believed that acting well demonstrated that they were among the elect. Eager to find such a sign in themselves, they

John Calvin was an important figure in Reformation theology, and one of the original proponents of the tradition later labelled Calvinism.

would eschew sin and depravity. The obvious counter-argument, made by the Dutch humanist Justus Velsius (*c*.1510–*c*.1581), is that if God has allowed some people to be born in the full knowledge that they are headed for eternal damnation and have no way of redeeming themselves, then He is a tyrant.

A more liberal view has God giving humans the ability to choose whether to act well or sinfully and then saving the good ones and letting the bad ones go to hell as they should. Because we are all, technically, damned because of original sin, He is being merciful in saving the good people rather than mean in damning the bad. God wrote the rules, of course, and damning unborn people because of someone else's sin long ago seems unreasonable.

'Let some suppose, from what has been said by us, that we say that whatever occurs happens by a fatal necessity, because it is foretold as known beforehand, this too we explain. We have learned from the prophets, and we hold it to be true, that punishments, chastisements, and good rewards, are rendered according to the merit of each man's actions. Now, if this is not so, but all things happen by fate, *then neither is anything at all in our own power. For if it is predetermined that this man will be good, and this other man will be evil, neither is the first one meritorious nor the latter man to be blamed. And again, unless the human race has the power of avoiding evil and choosing good by free choice, they are not accountable for their actions.'*

Justin Martyr, or St Justin (AD100–c.165)

NEUROLOGY AND FREE WILL

In 2008, a neurological experiment at the Max Planck Institute in Germany showed that test subjects' brain signals indicated which hand they were going to use in an experiment seven seconds before the subjects were conscious of having made the decision. It meant that researchers could predict the decision the subjects were going to make. This seemed to bring into question the issue of whether humans truly have freedom of choice in their decision-making. It appears that making a decision could be a physical consequence of something that is not an act of free will.

GOD'S NOT LOOKING

Baruch Spinoza saw everything as part of the One. As everything that happens is a necessary expression of the nature of the One, free will is effectively removed from humans. He maintained, however, that we experience life as though we are free:

'*Experience tells us clearly that men believe themselves to be free simply because they are conscious of their actions and unconscious of the causes whereby these actions are*

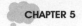
> *determined; further, it is plain that the dictates of the*
> *mind are simply another name for the appetites that vary*
> *according to the varying state of the body.'*

Spinoza said that each of us is ruled by our own emotions and appetites and hemmed in by limited understanding. Although we can't escape causal necessity, he suggested that if by reflection we can come to understand our place in the great causal chain, we can at least be freed from ignorance.

PHYSICAL DETERMINISM

The Ancient Greek philosopher Democritus believed that everything happened by necessity and was dictated by the predictable movement of atoms in the void. But he allowed that some atoms swerve in a way that is unpredictable, thus creating human souls and an element of freedom.

In some ways Democritus foreshadowed modern physics. He considered that all matter is made up of atoms ('uncuttables') and the properties of matter and behaviour of atoms mean that the progress of everything is predictable. Modern physics holds that everything can be predicted by physical laws (though we can't precisely predict the future, because our understanding of the physical laws is imperfect). This means we don't have free will unless we believe there is some non-physical animating spirit not subject to those laws. Anyone who subscribes to the view that consciousness is an emergent property of matter is left with the conclusion that we don't have free will – though we have the illusion of it. Without the illusion of free will, we would be frozen into inertia or driven to despair and existential angst.

How do we make a good life?

Some people live in such a way as to bring benefit only to themselves, regardless of the welfare of or cost to others. We tend to be judgemental about such people and describe their actions as selfish. But can we ever live a life that benefits all? And what do we mean by 'benefit' – a slippery term which is dependent on the individual concerned. For some, benefit is defined by maximizing pleasure and minimizing pain to the self. For others, the greatest benefit is salvation, which often involves renouncing physical pleasure. Meanwhile, others seek benefit from intellectual fulfilment or feeling at one with a universal spirit.

SOCRATES AND THE START OF ETHICS

The pre-Socratic philosophers were more concerned with 'meta-ethical' issues such as the nature of virtue than with the question of how to live virtuously. Socrates was the first to take a more practical interest in how we ought to live, and what a 'good life' might be – the concerns of normative ethics. He has been called the first philosopher of ethics, and his thinking has had a long-lasting and wide-ranging influence on Western ethical philosophy.

The doctrine of 'virtue ethics' began with Socrates, who believed that anyone who knows what virtue is will necessarily act well. If they know the difference between good and evil, they will choose the good course of action. He argued that knowledge (self-knowledge, in particular) is at the root of morality and that all crime and evil-doing are the result of ignorance about the real nature of virtue. As virtue leads to happiness, the wise person will be moral and therefore happy.

Socrates did not tell people how they should live, but encouraged them to examine their attitudes and ideas in the hope that this would have a beneficial effect on their behaviour. The difference between what a person ought to do, morally, and what a person might choose to do in his own interests was not so clear-cut in Ancient Greece as it is today. The Greeks believed that virtue was good both for the individual and for the community. They realized that living virtuously might not be the best way to prosper financially, but they didn't regard material wealth as a major factor in the success (or not) of a person's life.

Socrates' debating of ethical questions often led him into conflict with the elders of Athens, who accused him of corrupting the minds of the wealthy youth with revolutionary and unorthodox ideas. Although he left no written works, his ideas are recorded by his pupil Plato and demonstrated in the way he lived his life.

NORMATIVE ETHICS

Normative ethics deals with which actions are morally right and wrong. There are three main thrusts in the philosophy of normative ethics:

- *Virtue ethics focuses on the individual's moral intentions in acting.*
- *Deontology focuses on the rules regarding actions.*
- *Consequentialism focuses on the consequences of an action.*

STRIVING TOWARDS HAPPINESS

Aristotle's *Nichomachean Ethics* is one of the most important works on ethics in the history of Western philosophy. In it, he looked at how people should live, and how society should be organized, through laws and political structures, to enable virtuous living. He regarded happiness as a central purpose of human life and defined it as follows:

- As the ultimate end and purpose of human existence.
- Not as a pleasure or a virtue, but as the exercise of virtue.

- As a goal, not a temporary state, only achievable towards the end of a person's life.
- As the perfection of human nature through the exercise of reason.
- Through the acquisition of a moral character, where one displays the virtues of courage, generosity, justice, friendship and citizenship.
- Through intellectual contemplation.

For Aristotle, living a virtuous life went hand-in-hand with self-realization – with fulfilling one's potential, examining life and living thoughtfully. This accords with his general teleological approach: that everything is striving to fulfil its purpose. He saw virtue as striking a balance or 'golden mean' between an excess and a deficiency to achieve a middle path or 'settled condition of the soul'. For example, the virtue of courage is a mean regarding the feeling of fear, between a deficiency of fear (rashness) and an excess of fear (cowardice).

CYNICAL SELF-SUFFICIENCY

According to Plato, Diogenes of Sinope (see panel below) out-Socratesed Socrates; he was 'a Socrates gone mad'. A contemporary of Aristotle, it seems that Diogenes was both charismatic and enigmatic. No works by him survive, and it seems unlikely that he recorded his ideas in writing.

DIOGENES OF SINOPE (c.404–325BC)

Accounts of Diogenes' life are not wholly reliable, but they are entertaining. He was born in the Greek colony of Sinope on the Black Sea coast and worked with his father, Hicesias, a banker. He was exiled after being involved in a scandal to do with defacing coinage, and moved to Athens. Legend reports that he approached the philosopher Antisthenes, a pupil of Socrates, to be his tutor, but there is no real evidence that the two ever met.

Diogenes lived in a stone jar in the market place, making money by begging, and gave up as many possessions as he could. One anecdote says that after seeing a child scoop up water with his hands he broke his own drinking bowl in half as he realized that the bowl was a luxury he could do without.

When Plato quoted Socrates' definition of a man as a 'featherless biped', Diogenes is said to have responded by taking a plucked chicken to the Academy and presenting it as a man. Plato then revised the definition of a man to include 'broad, flat nails'.

According to legend, when Diogenes was in Corinth he witnessed the triumphal return of Alexander the Great. Intrigued by the fact that Diogenes took not the slightest notice of him, Alexander went to see the philosopher and found him lying on the ground. When Alexander asked if he wanted anything, Diogenes replied: 'Yes – stand a little out of my sun.'

Credited by some with originating the Cynic way of life, Diogenes distanced himself from the intellectual pretensions of other philosophers, adopting a straightforward and extremely ascetic approach to virtue. He believed that happiness was attained by living 'according to nature' and he strove to expose the falsity of society's conventional standards and beliefs by rejecting luxury and calling people back to a simple existence. Consequently, he lived in poverty, begged for his food and slept on the streets to demonstrate that happiness and independence were possible, even in straitened circumstances. Although he did not preach that everyone should live in this way, he claimed that in order to be fulfilled a person must give up all property, possessions, family ties and social values, as these are unnatural distractions.

Diogenes' anarchistic programme of self-sufficiency (the ability to possess within oneself all that one needs for happiness) also included the principles of 'shamelessness', or the ability to disregard convention and social ridicule, and 'outspokenness', or the uncompromising drive to expose vice and deceit wherever they were found.

> *'Those who have virtue always in their mouths, and neglect it in practice, are like a harp, which emits a sound pleasing to others, while itself is insensible of the music.'*
>
> Diogenes

SELF-REALIZATION REVISITED
Around 2,300 years after Aristotle, the French writer and philosopher Simone de Beauvoir worked to formulate a set of existential ethics in The Ethics of Ambiguity *(1947). She urged individuals first to recognize that they are free to become something different and that successful existence is then a process of 'becoming', marked by striving towards a desired identity.*

> *'The pursuit of pleasure is a life fit only for beasts.'*
>
> Aristotle, *Nicomachean Ethics*

Cynicism resurfaced in the 1st century, when cynics (ascetics) were found begging and preaching throughout the cities of the Roman Empire. There were good reasons for the movement's popularity. It coincided, both in Greece and Rome, with times of economic difficulty and social unrest. The idea that the one thing of real value is mastery of the self, which can't be taken away by misfortune, became attractive when material goods, social stability and family were all under threat.

CLEAR-THINKING CALM

Stoicism marked a similar but less extreme way of relinquishing temporal concerns. Beginning with Zeno of Citium (334–c.262BC) and continuing until the time of the Roman philosopher Seneca (4BC–AD65) and the Greek philosopher Epictetus (AD55–135), Stoicism taught a disdain for and disengagement from temporal woes and problems. It advised that destructive emotions (such as misery, envy and hate) are the result of errors in judgement. The way to happiness, open to the sage, is through moral and intellectual perfection. The goal of humankind is to live in accord with nature, which means to live by reason as we are all part of a universal, single, reasoning substance. The Stoics did not seek to deny or avoid emotions, but wanted to channel or transform them to produce, through self-discipline and reason, a clear-thinking calm.

Pragmatically, Seneca promoted a simple life devoted to virtue and reason, and insisted that the only good is virtue. He taught that doing the right thing is of paramount importance and that we each have an internal god guiding us along the path set out for us by providence. The only way to attain happiness is to follow this inner guide, acting in accord with our true nature, and being content with our lot. Altruism and simple living were essential to Seneca's idea of morality.

The Roman philosopher Boethius (AD480–c.525) was consoled by reading Seneca's writings while in prison. His own *Consolation of Philosophy* agrees with Seneca and the Stoics in promoting a disengagement or aloofness from the vicissitudes of fortune and a focus on reason and virtue. A Christian, Boethius wrote a Platonic and Stoic text that accorded with Christianity but did not mention the Christian God. As Boethius was both the last Roman philosopher and the first scholastic philosopher, his *Consolation* was something of a bridge between Seneca and Thomas Aquinas.

Boethius' Consolation of Philosophy, *written while he was in prison in 524, is the philosophical bridge between the ancient world and the Middle Ages. In this illustration, Lady Philosophy instructs Boethius on the role of God.*

AVOIDING PAIN

While Diogenes went to extremes to spurn worldly pleasures, Epicurus (342–270BC) taught the pursuit of happiness, which he considered to be achieved by avoiding physical and mental pain. He considered mental pain to be worse than physical pain, as the latter is temporary and can be brought under control or ends in death, at which point it no longer matters. (Epicurus didn't believe the soul persisted after death.) The mental pain of fear or anxiety, however, could continue unabated throughout a person's life. Epicurus believed that the root of human neurosis is death denial, and the tendency for humans to believe that death will be painful and terrible. Thus plagued with anxiety, he claimed, people would behave in selfish, hypocritical and unethical ways.

Even though Epicurus taught the pursuit of pleasure, he was not a hedonist as is mistakenly believed. He realized that over-indulgence could lead to painful consequences and therefore encouraged temperance. He taught that wisdom was the greatest virtue as it enables a person to distinguish between pleasures which should be sought and those which should be avoided. He believed that no one could be truly happy unless they were virtuous, as virtue leads to pleasurable consequences and to the absence of pain and fear.

EXTREMES OF PLEASURE
For true hedonism, we need to look to Aristippus of Cyrene (c.435–c.356BC), a wayward pupil of Socrates. The Cyrenaics believed in seeking pleasure from all experiences, where possible, and by maintaining proper control over both adverse and prosperous circumstances.

Ethics and Christianity

Although Boethius' *Consolation of Philosophy* is not an explicitly Christian work, it was immensely popular and influential throughout the Middle Ages. An accomplished scholar fully acquainted with Plato, Aristotle and his other predecessors, Boethius covers a lot of ground in the *Consolation*, including the issues of free will and predestination, the existence of evil and how to live a virtuous life. The book takes the form of a debate between Boethius and Lady Philosophy, who answers his tricky questions. Boethius is believed to have written the book while in prison awaiting his execution (for the charge of treason).

Throughout the Middle Ages, Christian philosophers had less flexibility of thought than their classical predecessors because the Bible is prescriptive about virtue and how people should live a good life. St Thomas Aquinas accommodated Aristotelian ethics into the Christian schema. He accepted Aristotle's teleological view that an act is good or bad depending on whether it contributes to or deters us from our proper human end – the *telos* or final goal to which all human actions aim. At the same time, he had to accept that ultimate fulfilment, for a Christian, is salvation and that can't be achieved by the individual alone – God's grace is required to perfect our nature.

BEING IS GOOD

St Augustine said 'things that exist are good', meaning that if something exists it must necessarily have some degree of goodness. He divided things into two categories, corruptible and incorruptible (incorruptible substances are superior to corruptible substances):

- An incorruptible substance cannot lose whatever goodness it may have.
- A corruptible substance *can* have some of its goodness removed.
- If a corruptible substance didn't have any goodness, it couldn't have any removed. Therefore, all corruptible substances have some goodness in them.

If a substance has no goodness, none can be removed, therefore it must be incorruptible. As incorruptibility is superior to corruptibility, it appears that something lacking goodness is preferable to something corruptible, which has goodness.

Clearly, this is nonsense – as St Augustine wrote, 'What can be more monstrous than to maintain that by losing all [its] goodness [something can] become better?'. He sidestepped the argument by concluding that there is some good in everything that exists.

Thomas Aquinas agreed, claiming that 'Goodness and being are really the same', whereas evil has no actuality in its own right. He said things can be more or less good (it is a relative term), but they either exist or they don't (it's an absolute). To address this problem, Aquinas came up with a type of being that he called 'relative being'. A thing 'is' more or less insofar as it is closer to the perfect essence of what that thing should be. So, for example, a hatchling is less of a bird than a fully-fledged bird, as it can't do all the things associated with full bird-ness such as flying, laying eggs, making nests, rearing young and so on. A fully-grown bird is therefore a 'better' bird than a hatchling. Similarly, a person is a better person if they act with morality, dignity and compassion than if they are selfish, immoral and cruel.

The same for all or different for each?

A code such as Christianity does not leave much space for individuals to come up with their own moral schema. For the 1,000 years or so following Boethius, Christian philosophers could do little with ethics. But by the 16th century, when the humanist Michel de Montaigne was writing, the Church was beginning to lose its iron grip.

Montaigne was the first philosopher to promote cultural relativism, which accepts that different behaviours and values are lauded in different cultures. There is no reason to suppose that one culture's way of doing things is better than another's or even that humans are innately superior to other animals. This was revolutionary thinking at the time, as Europeans exploited the general belief in their cultural superiority as an excuse for slaughtering, subjugating and indoctrinating the indigenous populations of North and South America, who were considered 'savages'. Of course, those who criticized the 'barbarous' practices of the 'savages' were often content to endorse or turn a blind eye to judicial torture in Europe.

Even so, Montaigne didn't believe all customs were equally acceptable, and nor were all individuals equally in thrall to their cultural norms. He urged every individual to examine what is expected in their social context and decide, based on universal and inherent standards bestowed by God, whether to accept the prevailing values. No universal code is necessary, as we can each look at different ways of doing things and make our own judgement about what is appropriate and best in any context. We should all, he felt, remain in constant dialogue and reflection to make the right choices.

CULTURAL RELATIVISM
Cultural relativism is the belief that values and moral or legal codes vary according to cultural context. What is acceptable in one culture may not be in another, and consequences follow from this. In Muslim countries, for example, some forms of Western dress are considered immodest.

'The laws of conscience, which we say are born of nature, are born of custom. Each man, holding in inward veneration the opinions and behaviour approved and accepted around him.'

Michel de Montaigne, *On Custom*

Montaigne accepted there were a few universal standards, such as 'reason' and 'nature', that were defined by God. These can help us to exercise our judgement. Montaigne's philosophy had an impact on Pascal and Descartes. Descartes, in particular, was heavily influenced by Montaigne's emphasis on self-education and the garnering of experience to inform philosophical reflection. This approach, devolving responsibility to the individual, is the hallmark of humanism. It does not preach either indulgence or asceticism as a route to self-discovery and virtue, but emphasizes the individual's own power and responsibility to find a path to a better life.

Immanuel Kant presented morality as an objective scheme which must be arrived at by 'pure practical reason'. Instead of each person assessing circumstances and custom and referring to their own moral compass, he believed that right and wrong are absolute and cannot be decided empirically, by referring to experience.

In *Critique of Practical Reason*, Kant explained what he called 'the categorical imperative'. This is a moral law or command that is unconditional for all agents, the validity or claim of which does not depend on any ulterior motive or end, for example: 'Do not kill.' This moral law applies to us simply because we possess rational wills, regardless of any personal objectives we might have. In Kant's words:

> *'Act only according to that maxim by which you can at the same time will that it should become a universal law.'*

Kant's categorical imperative states that moral duty should be entirely divorced from self-interest. As the quote implies, universal laws can be problematic – take, for example, those put in place by tyrants and dictators (who most definitely have an ulterior motive). History is littered with evidence that it requires watchfulness and sound judgement to ensure one person's ulterior motive doesn't become everyone else's universal law. Or, in Kant's words:

'So act as to treat humanity, whether in your own person or in another, always as an end, and never as only a means.'

Kant described any action based on desires as a 'hypothetical imperative', meaning a command of reason that applies only if we desire the goal in question. It requires us to exercise our will in a particular way given that we have an end in sight. It is a command in a conditional form, for example: 'If you want to do well in life, study hard.' It requires more than passively desiring an outcome; it means actively choosing or committing to an end.

Kant concludes that the only non-moral goal that we will is our own happiness. No rational imperatives can be issued for this end, because it is indeterminate. We can say we should save for the future, strive for a better job, form good relationships with our family, but as none of these guarantees happiness they are mere 'counsels' rather than commands.

The highest 'good', according to Kant, must be 'good in itself' (intrinsic good) and 'good without qualification'. The only good he found that fitted the criteria was 'good will': an act must be carried out with good will in order to be genuinely moral, and that means acting out of respect for the moral law. Insofar as Kant's interpretation of morality demands that people follow rules, it is deontological. There is an element of virtue ethics, though, in that virtuous intention must also be present.

Versions of Kant's theory of moral duty have been widely upheld and defended by philosophers right up to the present day.

> **DEONTOLOGICAL ETHICS**
> *A moral scheme based on duty is deontological (from* deon, *the Greek word for duty).*

In its uncompromising insistence on never using a person 'merely as a means to an end', Kant's scheme can be challenging (though not impossible) to implement. Some modern philosophers have tried to temper it to make it more viable. Harvard professor of philosophy Frances Kamm has described the 'principle of permissible harm' in which harm to a small number of people may be balanced against benefit to a large number of people under certain circumstances. So while it would be wrong in both Kamm's and Kant's scheme to kill someone to harvest their organs and save four other lives, it would be permissible in

In the Victorian children's story The Water Babies, *Mrs Doasyouwouldbedoneby is the embodiment of Kant's hypothetical imperative.*

Kamm's scheme to kill a gunman to save the people he was about to slaughter.

KANT AND THE GOLDEN RULE

Kant's hypothetical imperative is similar to the Golden Rule, or rule of reciprocity, that is found in most cultures and religions throughout the world. A general statement of it is: One should treat others as one would like others to treat oneself. There is also a negative form: One should not treat others in ways that one would not like to be treated. It is irrelevant how an individual might have been treated or might want to be treated; all that matters is whether the position could be extended to everyone without involving any contradiction. Kant's categorical imperative – in this instance, possibly, 'Do no harm' – is neither subjective nor hypothetical, it is absolute.

Utilitarian ethics

Kant's approach to ethics helped to wrest the issue away from religion, and this allowed a change of focus. Instead of acting morally in order to secure salvation (or to prove one's status as one of the elect), acting morally became part of a wider social responsibility.

The British social reformer Jeremy Bentham (1748–1832) is best known today as a political philosopher, but his political ideas overlap with his ideas about ethics. Born in Houndsditch, London, Bentham was a child prodigy who started to learn Latin at the age of three and went to Queen's College, Oxford at the age of 12. He trained as a lawyer and was called to the bar, but never practised – the over-complex language and conflicting principles of the law put him off. Instead, he undertook a philosophical investigation into the basis of law, morals and politics. Like Epicurus, Bentham believed that people are driven towards that which they desire (pleasure, or happiness) and avoid that which they fear (pain). By applying this principle to society, he developed and popularized a system known as 'utilitarianism'. He hoped to draw up a complete code of law based on utilitarian principles, which he called a 'Pannomion'.

The simple moral rule that emerges from Bentham's findings is that we should do whatever will maximize pleasure and minimize pain. Bentham's plan, though, is quantitative in nature: whatever brings the most pleasure to the most people is the best course of action, even though it may involve bringing pain to a few. Bentham did not shirk from quantifying pain and pleasure, and even developed a 'felicific calculus', an algorithm for calculating the sum total of pain and pleasure generated by an action or rule.

Sacrificing the few for the greater good: the graves of the Riley family, on a hillside above Eyam in Derbyshire, UK. The village is famous for quarantining its population in an attempt to contain the spread of the Great Plague in 1665–6.

> 'It is the greatest happiness of the greatest number that is the measure of right and wrong.'
>
> Jeremy Bentham, *A Fragment on Government* (1776)

> 'Nature has placed mankind under the governance of two sovereign masters, pain and pleasure. . . . They govern us in all we do, in all we say, in all we think: every effort we can make to throw off our subjection will serve but to demonstrate and confirm it. In words, a man may pretend to abjure their empire, but in reality he will remain subject to it all the while.'
>
> Jeremy Bentham, *An Introduction to the Principles of Morals and Legislation* (1789)

Bentham was not the first person to express the idea that the morality of an action can be measured by how much pleasure or pain it brings to people. In *An Inquiry into the Original of Our Ideas of Beauty and Virtue* (1725), the philosopher Francis Hutcheson wrote:

> 'that action is best, which procures the greatest happiness for the greatest numbers; and that, worst, which, in like manner, occasions misery.'

He, too, offered algorithms 'to compute the Morality of any Actions'. His contemporary, John Gay, took the idea a step further in 1731, claiming that it is the will of God that people should be happy and therefore we are obliged by religion to pursue the path that will lead to the greatest pleasure for the greatest number.

Taken to extremes, utilitarianism could allow the life of one person to be sacrificed to bring pleasure to many, though Bentham ruled against this by allowing that the legal system would protect individuals against such an abuse. The law, he said,

'provides the basic framework of social interaction by delimiting spheres of personal inviolability within which individuals can form and pursue their own conceptions of well-being'.

The jury is still out on whether or not this is true in practice.

DEAD, BUT NOT GONE

As he requested in his will, Bentham's body was dissected as part of a public anatomy lecture and his skeleton formed into an 'auto-icon' padded with straw and dressed in his clothes (see photo). The shoddy mummification of his head produced a macabre result and a wax effigy, embellished with his own hair, was used instead. The auto-icon usually sits in the south cloisters of the main building of University College London but has, on occasion, attended meetings of the college council, recorded as 'present but not voting'. Bentham's mummified head, originally displayed in the same case as the auto-icon, is now locked in a secure location.

'The day may come when the rest of the animal creation may acquire those rights which never could have been witholden from them but by the hand of tyranny. The French have already discovered that the blackness of the skin is no reason a human being should be abandoned without redress to the caprice of a tormentor. It may one day come to be recognized that the number of the legs, the villosity [hairiness] of the skin, or the termination of the os sacrum [end of the spine] are reasons equally insufficient for abandoning a sensitive being to the same fate. . . . The question is not, Can they reason? nor, Can they talk? but, Can they suffer?'

Jeremy Bentham, *Introduction to the Principles of Morals and Legislation* (1789)

One of Bentham's students, John Stuart Mill (1806–73), developed the 'greatest happiness' principle further, both in ethics and politics. He divided pleasure into higher and lower categories. According to Mill, the higher pleasures are intellectual, sophisticated and cultural while the lower pleasures are carnal and physical:

'If I am asked what I mean by difference of quality in pleasures, or what makes one pleasure more valuable than another, merely as a pleasure, except its being greater in amount, there is but one possible answer. If one of the two is, by those who are competently acquainted with both, placed so far above the other that they prefer it, even though knowing it to be attended with a greater amount of discontent, and would not

resign it for any quantity of the other pleasure which their nature is capable of, we are justified in ascribing to the preferred enjoyment a superiority in quality so far outweighing quantity as to render it, in comparison, of small account.'

'No reason can be given why the general happiness is desirable, except that each person, so far as he believes it to be attainable, desires his own happiness.'

John Stuart Mill, *Utilitarianism*

How do we choose?

The English philosopher and economist Henry Sidgwick (1838–1900) explored the methods of everyday moral reasoning – how we arrive at decisions about moral behaviour, and whether there can be a rational basis on which to make such decisions. His book *The Methods of Ethics* (1874) became one of the classics of moral philosophy.

Sidgwick considered a 'method of ethics' to be

'any rational procedure by which we determine what individual human beings "ought" to do – or what it is "right" for them to do – or to seek to realize by voluntary action.'

Of course, people follow different principles when deciding what to do, but he said their 'methods' can be grouped according to three basic approaches: egoism, utilitarianism and intuitionism.

Egoism, or egoistic hedonism, deems an action to be more or less moral depending on how happy it makes the person performing it:

> '*The rational agent regards quantity of consequent pleasure and pain to himself as alone important in choosing between alternatives of action; and seeks always the greatest attainable surplus of pleasure over pain.*'

Utilitarianism measures the morality of an action according to its effect on the general happiness of all:

> '*The conduct which . . . is objectively right, is that which will produce the greatest amount of happiness on the whole . . . taking into account all whose happiness is affected by the conduct.*'

Intuitionism takes the view that we can understand instinctively, through our intuitive awareness, which actions are moral in themselves. It is usually taken as essential that there is self-evident or *a priori* moral knowledge. In the 19th century, intuitionism was considered by many philosophers to be a rival of utilitarianism. But as Sidgwick examined the relationship between intuitionism and the 'morality of common sense', the ethical guidelines that guide people's everyday behaviour, he found that common-sense morality is to some extent 'unconsciously utilitarian'. Utilitarianism rests on intuitive moral principles. Sidgwick concluded that intuitionism and utilitarianism can be integrated into a single ethical system:

> '*Such abstract moral principles as we can admit to be really self-evident . . . seem to be required to furnish a rational basis for [a utilitarian] system.*'

Although he had reconciled these two methods, egoism remained outside the fold. Egoism also seems to reflect reason and common sense, but it is the opposite of utilitarianism, which might require a person to sacrifice their own happiness, or even their own life, for the greater happiness of society.

> 'It is better to be a human being dissatisfied than a pig satisfied; better to be Socrates dissatisfied than a fool satisfied. And if the fool, or the pig, are of a different opinion, it is because they only know their own side of the question.'
>
> John Stuart Mill, *Utilitarianism* (1861)

Sidgwick acknowledged that few people are as concerned with the pleasure or pain of humankind generally as with that of themselves and their nearest and dearest. He was left with two conflicting principles, utilitarianism and egoism, which are irreconcilable but both based on common sense and valid reasoning. When utilitarian reason makes harsh demands on us, self-interested reason might rightly lead us to oppose it. Sidgwick admitted that the conflict remains insoluble without the involvement of God and some notion of divine reward and punishment, but he was unwilling to resort to religion to dig himself out of this particular hole. He ended the first edition of his book on a despairing note:

> 'The prolonged effort of the human intellect to frame a perfect ideal of rational conduct is seen to have been foredoomed to inevitable failure.'

Starting over

Friedrich Nietzsche saw a similar failure in the moral codes that had so far evolved. His answer to the problem was to overturn all existing moral structures and start afresh. He located the fundamental driving force of the individual in the need to dominate and control external forces and take charge of personal destiny; yet for many people life circumstances prevent them from doing this. According to Nietzsche, the moral codes that have evolved have done so as a result of trying to accommodate our inability to take control and be self-determining, or even to avoid acknowledging it. They exist to bind and control the striving will of the individual.

Nietzsche traced the predominant moral schemas of Europe, whether classical or Christian, to the behaviour of masters and slaves, or overlords and the oppressed. Moral good and evil are based on the values admired by those who have the upper hand in society (the masters), which are seen as either desirable (by the masters) or evil (by the slaves). In Homeric Greece and other societies marked by a master-slave dichotomy or hierarchical class structure, the life-affirming attributes such as power, physical strength, health and wealth are considered good by those in power. The opposite characteristics are life-denying: poverty, powerlessness, sickness, and so on. Nietzsche describes this schema as master-morality, though strictly speaking there is no moral position assigned to the characteristics labelled as good or bad – they are rather desirable and undesirable states or properties.

It is not the masters, but the slaves who give the system an evaluation based on what is 'moral' or not. The underclass is forced to adopt certain characteristics in order to explain their oppressed state. Therefore, cruelty, worldliness, selfishness, aggression and wealth are seen as evil, and humility, poverty, selflessness, submission and piety are seen as morally good. (The masters take the opposite view of what constitutes bad and good characteristics, of course.) By re-labelling the marks of their powerlessness as virtues, the slaves are able to endure their lot, but also avoid the obligation to remedy it.

A warped version of Nietzsche's philosophy, which saw the demise of Christianity and the rise of individual power as a force for good, was appropriated by the leaders of Nazi Germany.

Nietzsche saw the tension between master- and slave-moralities as the cause of rising nihilism in Christian Europe. 'God is dead,' he said, suggesting that nihilism had triumphed, or will triumph. Religious belief was, he felt, a bulwark against nihilism, and without it we struggle to find meaning or to forge a moral code. Nihilism leads easily to despair. But it is also the first step towards a culture with solid foundations, since that depends on overcoming nihilism:

> *'I praise, I do not reproach [nihilism's] arrival. I believe it is one of the greatest crises, a moment of the deepest self-reflection of humanity. Whether man recovers from it, whether he becomes master of this crisis, is a question of his strength!'*

Nietzsche hoped that the foundations of the new morality could be built amid the rubble of Christianity and nihilism. But, for Nietzsche, there was no absolute moral law.

Nietzsche maintained that the value systems which societies produce vary according to their own circumstances and needs, and none is intrinsically better than any other. He believed it was the act of developing and adhering to a code of values that was the important point, the defining act of a civilized society, and not the content of that code. This view, called 'perspectivism', was adopted by some later philosophers, including Martin Heidegger, who developed it into full cultural relativism.

Meta-ethics

From the middle of the 19th century, the Christian fabric of Europe began to unravel more rapidly. Since the Enlightenment, serious thinkers had begun to question the belief in the God they had been raised to worship and although many, after careful examination, retained their faith, an increasing number rejected it or found it did not answer their needs. Those who, like Spinoza, arrived at a different type of theism had to rethink morality. Those who, like Nietzsche, cast off religion altogether as oppressive and misguided needed a completely new basis for morality.

This chapter has been largely concerned with normative ethics – how people should behave. But the beginning of the 20th century saw philosophy taking a step backwards, away from normative ethics, and trying to gain an overview with 'meta-ethics' – an investigation of what we mean when we talk about right and wrong and how we can make moral judgements.

The English philosopher G. E. Moore (1873–1958) rejected metaphysical theories in favour of common-sense realism. So, for example, you or I can more readily accept that we existed yesterday than that we need someone like Descartes to help us prove we existed yesterday. Moore – like many people – thought a lot of philosophy was unnecessary nonsense. Many questions about meaning are not asked in everyday life, though the relationship between concepts and their definitions is important in philosophy. In this, he sparked some of the major themes of 20th-century philosophy, including the preoccupation with language.

'It seems plain that a truth differs in no respect from the reality to which it was supposed merely to correspond: e.g. the truth that I exist differs in no respect from the corresponding reality – my existence. So far, indeed, from truth being defined by reference to reality, reality can only be defined by reference to truth.'

G. E. Moore, 'Truth', 1900

In *Principia Ethica* (1903), Moore is concerned with the meta-ethical question of what we mean by 'good' rather than which actions might be deemed to be good. He says that 'good' can't be broken down, but is

'a simple notion, just as "yellow" is a simple notion. Just as you cannot, by any manner of means, explain to anyone who does not already know it, what yellow is, so you cannot explain what good is.'

'Good', said Moore, is something of which we are intuitively aware. We know it is good to be kind to other people and bad to be cruel to them. We don't really need an explanation of why, so he rejects the utilitarian view as well as Kant's conclusion that ethical judgements are accessible to reason. A judgement of what

Can it ever be ethical to assassinate violent dictators, such as Saddam Hussein?

is 'good' is always subjective, a value judgement. On the whole, people tend to agree a lot of the time. We disagree over points of detail, of course. We might all agree that it's wrong to kill people. Some people will hold the view, however, that judicial killing is acceptable or that abortion is acceptable or that euthanasia is acceptable. These details are the material of 'applied ethics'. Because good cannot be defined acceptably, Moore concluded that ethics can have no basis in either science or metaphysics.

Ethics in daily life

Applied ethics, the application of ethics to everyday life, is what we are engaged in when asking questions such as 'do animals have rights?' or 'should we assassinate dictators?' The 20th century saw a proliferation of works on specific areas such as bioethics, animal rights and business ethics.

The usual methods of normative ethics (virtue ethics, deontological ethics and utilitarian ethics) approach ethical questions from very different starting points. One of the consequences of the fragmentation in theoretical moral codes has been that there are many accepted but often conflicting viewpoints in modern society. The work of ethics committees and other bodies concerned with making ethical judgements is harder now than it would have been at a time when a universal moral order imposed by the Bible held sway.

One way of dealing with the plurality of theoretical positions is to adopt a method of case-based reasoning, called casuistry. It has its origins in Aristotle, and was briefly popular in the 16th and 17th centuries. Moore was sympathetic towards casuistry:

> *'Casuistry is the goal of ethical investigation. It cannot be safely attempted at the beginning of our studies, but only at the end.'*

After more than half a century of post-Moorean philosophy, casuistry resurfaced in the 1960s as a usable method in applied ethics, and became more prevalent following the publication of a ground-breaking work, *The Abuse of Casuistry: A History of Moral Reasoning* (1988), by the American biomedical ethicist Albert Jonsen (born 1931) and the British philosopher Stephen Toulmin (1922–2009). This study tackles each individual case in the context of its own circumstances. It works from the known facts and likely consequences, rather than starting from a theoretical code (though it still has to operate within the law). An example of its application is in deciding whether to withdraw life-support from a very sick patient. Because it is not rule-based, it can result in opposite rulings on cases that look very similar.

ETHICAL RESISTANCE – ETHICS FOR THE 21ST CENTURY

Post-structuralist and post-modernist philosophers denied the possibility of an objective or even a subjective moral code, saying that all actions must be seen in their own context and in relation to others. In practice, this produces casuistry, with each case judged independently of a moral schema. David Couzens

Hoy, professor of philosophy at the University of California, Santa Cruz, identified an 'ethical turn' in philosophy in the 1980s and 1990s. He describes modern ethics as 'obligations that present themselves as necessarily to be fulfilled but are neither forced on one or are enforceable'. Hoy sees acts such as rejecting consumerism in favour of simpler ways of living, or boycotting businesses that avoid paying tax, as examples of 'ethical resistance' – a way for the powerless to push back against the powerful. The powerless can be any group, human or not, including the poor, the unborn, animals and marginalized ethnic or sexual groups.

The good life

The consensus of the last two millennia seems to be that living a good, morally virtuous life is likely to produce happiness. This will not result in material wealth because, in many cases, selfish and immoral behaviour has a better chance of producing more material wealth. But it will at least enable us, as individuals, to feel true to ourselves, free from guilt and shame.

Living virtuously is not dependent on religion. Although religion may offer people a blueprint for virtuous living, and the faithful often claim a monopoly on morality, the drive to goodness is in all – or most – of us. Living well is, in Aristotle's terms, the way to become a fully realized human, fulfilling one's natural purpose.

'The ethical resistance of the powerless others to our capacity to exert power over them is therefore what imposes unenforceable obligations on us. The obligations are unenforceable precisely because of the other's lack of power. That actions are at once obligatory and at the same

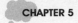

time unenforceable is what put them in the category of the ethical. Obligations that were enforced would, by the virtue of the force behind them, not be freely undertaken and would not be in the realm of the ethical.'

David Couzens Hoy, *Critical Resistance: From Poststructuralism to Postcritique* (2004)

How do we make a good society?

—

'*I am not an Athenian or a Corinthian,*
but a citizen of the world.'
Diogenes of Sinope (according to Epictetus, *Discourses*)

'*That to secure these Rights, Governments are instituted*
among Men. . . . Whenever any Form of Government

becomes destructive of these Ends, it is the Right of the
People to alter or to abolish it.'
Thomas Jefferson,
United States Declaration of Independence (1776)

The two philosophical questions of 'how do you live a good
life?' and 'how do you make a good society?' are inextricably
linked, but philosophers have differed in their view of the
degree to which ethics should dictate policy or the legal code.
The Italian politician and diplomat Niccolò Machiavelli
(1469–1527) took an entirely pragmatic approach – the
opposite of Bentham's proposed revision of the legal code
along ethical grounds.

So who should set out the law, and how should it be
enforced? What gives a government legitimacy? What form
should a government take? What are the obligations of a
government towards its citizens and what duties do citizens
owe their government and country? And finally, is it ever right
to overthrow a government?

IS THE WHOLE OTHER THAN THE SUM OF ITS PARTS?

*There are, broadly speaking, two approaches to political
philosophy. The individualist approach sees societies as
the sum of the individuals within them. The collectivist
approach sees society as more than a collection of people,
as something that has its own autonomy and identity.
The rights of the individual are less important in the
collectivist view.*

The Prince, by Niccolò Machiavelli, has been used as a reference manual by many political leaders, including Joseph Stalin.

The social contract

In some ways, political philosophy is the practical application of metaphysics. It involves defining concepts such as justice, freedom, authority and fairness and then finding social structures in which they can be implemented.

The idea that there is a social contract between the individual and society first surfaces in Plato's work and persists to the present day. In Plato's *Crito*, the character of Socrates says he has entered into a contract with the city of Athens by remaining there as a adult; as part of that contract, he is bound by the city's laws and by its judgement of him. As a consequence of entering into that contract, he must accept the punishment of execution, even if he feels it was handed down unjustly.

THE GOOD OF THE STATE

Plato's *The Republic* (*c.*380BC) is the first substantial work of political philosophy. It describes a utopian society led by an elite class of guardians who are trained from birth to rule. The rest of society is divided into soldiers and the common people. In the republic, the ideal citizens are those who understand how best to use their talents to benefit society, and do precisely what is needed to achieve that. Everything is organized for the good of the state as a whole, with little regard for personal freedom or individual rights. Such a society, Plato believed, would be just to all its citizens, giving to and taking from each as is their due. It would also be invincible because its structure would make it much stronger than any of its enemies.

The Republic extends Plato's idea of 'Forms' to the realm of politics. It describes the ideal society, of which all existing societies are only imperfect approximations or copies. No existing society (in Plato's time or now) manages to promote the good of all citizens – a feature of the ideal.

The vision of society portrayed in *The Republic* has been criticized extensively over the last 2,300 years. With the benefit of hindsight and historical perspective, the British philosopher Bertrand Russell accused Plato of endorsing an elitist and totalitarian regime under the guise of communist or socialist principles. After the spectacular failure of an assortment of communist and fascistic totalitarian regimes during the 20th century, the ideal society appeared to be nothing more than a pipe dream. Plato's model seems not to have allowed for the brutish and cold-blooded desire of some humans to dominate others.

THE FOUR OPTIONS
There are four broadly distinct political positions:
Liberalism *inclines towards equality and freedom for all, but the inherent problem of people being personally unequal (in intelligence, for instance) leads to an equality of opportunity or resources being the best that can be achieved.*
Conservatism *distrusts wholesale revision and believes that practices which don't work will slowly die out on their own. Conservatism trusts everything to find its own level, including the market (economy) – hence an adherence to free-market capitalism.*

Socialism believes that resources are better used and managed if owned collectively so that individual bias or ambition cannot operate to the detriment of the whole of society. There may be moral or practical reasons for approving of state ownership.

Anarchism holds that people cannot live a good life, the definition of which is different for different individuals, if they are constrained by a hierarchy or set of limitations. The difficulty for anarchy is in recognizing which structures are naturally emerging and may form part of a good life, and which are imposed.

THE CONSTITUTION AS SOUL

Plato's pupil, Aristotle, severely criticized *The Republic*. Employed by Philip II of Macedon as personal tutor to the boy who would later become Alexander the Great, Aristotle had witnessed high-level politics at first hand. His *Politics* gives advice to rulers and statesmen based on his view that the role of political leaders is to frame the laws or constitution, then maintain and revise them as necessary. He believed the natural function of man is to act according to reason based in virtue, and that this should be harnessed and recognized in political structures.

Aristotle saw the relationship between the constitution and the city-state as equivalent to that of a soul in a living organism. The city-state is made up of a particular population in a specific territory with a constitution that defines its aims. The aim of the properly constituted city-state is the happiness of its citizens. Aristotle's *Politics* discusses the ideal city-state, and classifies and discusses the merits and demerits of various types of government.

Aristotle believed that humans naturally come together to form societies (a doctrine called political naturalism) and that they are political animals. His definition of a 'citizen', however, is rather narrow as it excludes women, slaves, children and foreigners. Only full citizens are permitted to play a part in the running of the city-state.

His analysis of the different forms of government divided them into just (correct) and unjust (deviant) forms, adapted from Plato:

	Correct	Deviant
A single ruler	Monarchy	Tyranny
Minority rule	Aristocracy	Oligarchy
Majority rule	Polity (democracy)	Ochlocracy (mob rule)

Although Aristotle considered a ruler who exerts absolute power over citizens to be a tyrant, he saw no problem with exerting absolute power over slaves, women or children. He considered women and children to be of reduced rational capacity and in need of guidance, and 'natural' slaves lacking in direction and needing a master rather than being left to their own devices.

Justice, according to Aristotle, requires that individuals receive benefits in proportion to their merit or deserts. The city-state is neither a business enterprise to maximize wealth (as the oligarchs suppose) nor an association to promote liberty and equality (as the democrats maintain). Instead, its aim is 'the good life', which is a life consisting of noble actions. The ideal constitution is one in which the citizens are fully virtuous.

Aristotle criticized Plato's *The Republic* for being too concerned with the city-state rather than the individual citizens, and for promoting an approach that is counter to human nature. His own recommendations were more pragmatic. Although he theorized about an ideal constitution, he acknowledged that most lawgivers are not in a position to institute the ideal, so will have to make compromises.

In practical terms, the best government often turns out to be government by the many. For Aristotle, government by the middle classes was often preferable to government by a handful of rich people. Both the rich and the poor are inclined to make bad decisions because they are motivated by personal feelings and interests, while the middle classes are more likely to be moderate. The notion that society should be governed by many citizens with individual merits, whose collective merits benefit society as a whole, is one that underpins many modern constitutions.

Aristotle covered in depth many of the enduring concerns of political philosophy: the role of human nature, ideals and morality in practical politics; the relation of the individual to the state; the theory of justice; the rule of law; constitutions; and the causes of revolution.

> 'Since we see that every city-state is a sort of community and that every community is established for the sake of some good (for everyone does everything for the sake of what they believe to be good), it is clear that every community aims at some good, and the community which has the most authority of all and includes all the others aims highest, that is, at the good with the most authority. This is what is called the city-state or political community.'
>
> Aristotle, *Politics*

THE STOICS AND EQUALITY

Seneca, a free-minded Stoic writing later in Rome, was also concerned with moral issues, as his 124 letters attest. He regarded philosophy as a curative balm for the wounds inflicted by life, and explored subjects such as self-control, mortality, poverty and the uses of wealth. He had an enlightened attitude towards slavery, writing around AD65:

> 'Please remember that the person you call your slave rose from the same seeds, enjoys the same sky and equally breathes, lives and dies! You could see him just as much as a free man as a slave.'

The Stoics held that all people are naturally born equal. This belief is not very convenient for most rulers, of course, and it disappeared from political philosophy for a long time.

A convert to Stoicism, the Roman emperor Marcus Aurelius (AD121–180) was something of a personal contradiction. Although in his *Meditations* he showed concern for the social problems of the poor, slaves and the imprisoned, as emperor he continued to persecute the Christian population. The *Meditations* are a collection of aphorisms which present his ideas on ethics and politics.

As a philosophy, Stoicism encouraged people to accept the moment as it presents itself and to resist being controlled by the desire for pleasure or fear of pain. It taught that a person should use his/her mind to understand the world and work to treat others fairly and justly – a central tenet being that 'virtue is the only good'. The Stoics believed that the best indication of an individual's character was not in what they said, but how they behaved. They also held that the laws of the natural order were paramount and that everything was rooted in nature.

> 'Freedom is secured not by the fulfilling of men's desires, but by the removal of desire.'
>
> Epictetus (AD55–135)

Marcus Aurelius was a Stoic philosopher and Roman emperor. He was co-emperor with Lucius Verus from 161–169 and ruled alone from 169–180.

BRINGING GOD TO THE CITY

St Augustine was born and died in North Africa, though he spent some time in Rome and Milan. A convert to Christianity in his early thirties, he devoted himself to trying to show that reason upheld faith.

While Augustine tried to reconcile Christian thinking with the writings of Plato, and Thomas Aquinas did the same with the writings of Aristotle, medieval Christian philosophers paid little attention to the issue of politics independently of this legacy. There was a tendency to dismiss politics as not really their concern. Rendering unto Caesar that which is Caesar's seems to have included temporal power and political matters. Augustine wrote that the Christian community was a spiritual community, not a political community. Aquinas, writing 800 years later, identified four levels of law, with God's divine law at the top and temporal human law at the bottom. It was not until the Renaissance, with its turmoil and intellectual advances, that political theory re-emerged as an important philosophical concern.

THE DEVIL YOU KNOW . . .

Born in Florence during a time of devious machinations between the great Italian ruling families, Niccolò Machiavelli was the most influential political philosopher of the Renaissance. His greatest work, *The Prince* (1532), was presented as a guide to rulers, giving a detailed analysis of successful political techniques. Machiavelli took an amoral stance, refusing to rule out means that many political scientists would regard as too extreme. For him, pragmatism was the ultimate deciding factor. Tyranny was denigrated not because it is immoral but because it arouses dangerous enemies. Machiavelli's advice that it can be useful for a ruler to appear virtuous in order to gain support has led to his name becoming shorthand for scheming, duplicitous practice and the pursuit of pragmatism in politics.

In order to be effective, Machiavelli believes the prince should strive for three goals: national security, independence and a strong political constitution. In Machiavelli's view, the ends justify the means as long as the ends are worthwhile, and this remains more or less true regardless of the means employed to attain them. Machiavelli advises princes to follow their convictions with strength and courage and to act unscrupulously should the situation require it.

Most of Machiavelli's practical advice relates to manipulating people – supporters, allies, the populace and other rulers – in order to attain and retain power. To be an outright tyrant is generally a bad move because it is antagonistic and makes ruling more difficult and the prince's position insecure. A prince needs to create the conditions for a reasonably content population as such people are easy to govern and won't battle to overthrow him; for this reason alone it is sensible to deal fairly, if firmly, with the populace. In his *Discourses* (*c*.1517), Machiavelli says the most successful form of government is a republic run by princes but held in check by the nobility and ordinary citizens.

THE 'JUST WAR' PROBLEM

A problem in political philosophy which has been of recent interest in the West is that of the 'just war'. This notion was introduced by St Augustine in his work on Christian philosophy, The City of God. *Plato had said that 'justice is in the interest of the stronger' (a version of 'right is might'). Augustine divided the issue into two questions: 'Is it right to go to war?' and 'What actions are allowable in a war?' He required that four main conditions be met for a war to be considered moral:*

1. *Just authority – the decision to go to war must be based on a legitimate political and legal process.*
2. *Just cause – war is the most appropriate response to a wrong that has been committed.*
3. *Right intention – the war action is limited to righting the wrong (no 'mission creep' is allowed).*
4. *Last resort – other avenues having been explored, war is the only remaining option.*

Furthermore, an army must only use force in proportion to the cause and must not do more than is necessary to correct the wrong suffered; an army must not attack innocent, non-combatant civilians; an army is not responsible for unforeseen bad consequences as long as the good of war outweighs the bad and the war is carried out with good intentions.

Augustine set out his guidelines at a time when the Roman Empire was in decline and falling to other powers. The question of the morality of war was of immediate and urgent importance, and has remained so to this day.

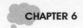

PERFECT WORLDS

Several philosophers have followed Plato in setting out their blueprint for a perfect society as a utopia – an ideal state. The social philosopher and statesman Sir Thomas More (1478–1535) called his visionary land 'Utopia' (from the Greek *eutopos*, meaning 'good place') and described it in a book of the same name. For many years More was a trusted adviser to Henry VIII, but the king had him executed in 1535 because, as a devout Catholic, More would not endorse Henry's divorce, remarriage and appointment as the head of the new Church of England.

UTOPIA

'Utopia' has become a generic term for an ideal, imaginary state with a perfect constitution and society.

Utopia (1516) is presented as a dialogue between More himself and a traveller, Raphael Hythloday, who has just returned after living for five years on the island of Utopia in the South Seas. Utopia is essentially a socialist state, with communal property, great productivity, where there is no personal ambition or commerce and there is little inclination to war. Nearly everyone is equal. The exceptions are the bondsmen who carry out the most unpleasant tasks; these are either criminals or foreigners under sentence of death. Everyone works six days a week, wears the same clothes and lives in identical houses, which they have to swap regularly to discourage the residents from customizing or becoming too attached to them. The towns are all built to a regular plan, people eat communally and everyone has everything they need.

'Life in More's Utopia, as in most others, would be intolerably dull. Diversity is essential to happiness, and in Utopia there is hardly any.'

Bertrand Russell

One way in which Utopia is very different from the oppressive communist regimes of the 20th century is in its religious tolerance: all religions are tolerated, but atheism is not. More held that a godless citizen could not be trusted to recognize any other authority and therefore would not be governable.

Intellectuals and governors are chosen on merit in Utopia and stay in post only for as long as they are able to perform their duties well. They can't inherit the position or continue in it if

Sir Thomas More, considered a saint by the Catholic Church, was executed for opposing the divorce of King Henry VIII.

indigent or lazy. The head of state is an elected prince who can be removed if he turns out to be a tyrant.

In *Utopia*, More was able to depict an alternative view of society without openly criticizing Henry VIII's England. He used the book to articulate socialist ideals completely unfamiliar and unvoiced in Tudor England. Whether he believed that Utopia was a possible or even desirable society is not clear, but many other authors took their cue from him and wrote about other imaginary societies. Shakespeare's late play *The Tempest* (1623) tackles a similar theme, with the magician Prospero creating an island paradise for himself and Miranda, his daughter.

Natural man and natural law

During the 17th and 18th centuries, influential philosophical thinkers turned their attention to the laws of society and the type of social contract humankind makes in order to form them. One of Aquinas' four levels of law was 'natural law' – rules produced by the application of reason. The idea of natural law and how humans would behave in a 'natural' state became a focus of interest for several political philosophers. They had very different ideas about what constituted a 'natural' (non-civic) state, as this was a condition that was almost impossible to witness first hand. Travellers' tales of native peoples inhabiting newly discovered lands such as the Americas or Australia fed information of dubious reliability into the debate.

THE LAWS OF THE UNIVERSE APPLIED TO SOCIETY

Like Descartes, the English philosopher Thomas Hobbes (1596–1650) looked to developments in science in order to develop a philosophical model. If, as Galileo and Newton had demonstrated, the universe worked according to a set of natural rules, why shouldn't this also be the case for social structures? Hobbes applied the rule of natural law to the realm of politics.

Thomas Hobbes believed that humans, left to their own devices and with no social structure, would resort to selfish and destructive behaviour.

His first treatise on political science, *Elements of Law*, was distributed to supporters of Charles I in 1640 to justify the king's actions to an increasingly hostile parliament. Hobbes spent the next ten years in self-imposed exile in France, where he first developed his defence of a king's right to rule as an absolute monarch in *De Cive* (1642). He revisited the topic at length in his masterpiece, *Leviathan* (1651).

Leviathan begins with the assumption that all people naturally seek their own selfish ends and that if this instinct is left unchecked, social chaos will result. To avoid constant battles between themselves, people willingly surrender their individual rights to the authority of a ruler, either a monarch or a governing assembly, which Hobbes calls a sovereign. In return, the sovereign ensures the well-being and security of the people. Put another way, the natural state of humankind is one of war and strife, and only the rules of social living, imposed by force, prevent us from falling back into that natural state. Without the covenant between individuals and the sovereign, Hobbes says, society would disintegrate and it would be 'a war of every man, against every man' and each person's life would be 'solitary, poor, nasty, brutish and short'.

The social contract prevents humankind from reverting to this state and works because it offers safety and sufficient of what we need – so although every individual is still self-interested, each person's needs are met in a way that takes account of everyone else's needs.

NOT ALL BAD

John Locke also believed that human nature is essentially selfish, but he considered it to be mediated by reason and tolerance. He argued that in their 'natural state' people had a right to protect their 'life, health, liberty, or possessions' and their first instinct was to work together to resolve conflicts and defend rights in a civil way. This common-sense argument assumed that humans would find it easier to defend such rights as a group than as isolated individuals. Locke saw the creation and accumulation of property as initially limited; people had to work to produce goods, which were generally perishable.

The introduction of a monetary system enabled people to keep producing and swapping perishable goods for something that endures and retains its value, therefore removing the limit on accumulation. Locke believed in market forces and wrote that the value of anything rises and falls according to how much is available and how many people want it (supply and demand). He saw money as a positive force, since it could prevent waste, and he considered unused property to be a waste and an offence against nature. Locke believed social inequality was the result of a tacit agreement societies make about how to use money. He recognized it was the job of governments to introduce rules that would moderate the conflict between unlimited accumulation and equal distribution, but didn't consider it his task to think about how this might be achieved.

Locke supported constitutional monarchy as the ideal form of government but denied the divine right of kings (the idea that a king is given his position by God and therefore may not be overthrown). In *Two Treatises of Government* (1690) he argued against hereditary power and an absolute monarchy, claiming that a government is only legitimate if ruled with the consent of the citizens. He believed that both parts of the social contract must be upheld: the people must obey the rulers, but the rulers have a duty to support and nurture the citizens.

THE NOBLE SAVAGE

Jean-Jacques Rousseau considered the natural state of humans to be innately good: 'Men in a state of nature do not know good and evil, but only their independence.' This natural knowledge, along with 'the peacefulness of their passions, and their ignorance of vice, prevents them from doing ill', he optimistically argued.

Rousseau's approach laid all humanity's ills at the door of the social structures we have built. The entire Romantic movement, in philosophy, art, literature and music, stems from Rousseau's belief that the innate state of humankind is one of nobility and natural grandeur and that the closer we can be to our nature (and to Nature itself) the better we will live.

Rousseau set out his ideas for creating a perfect society in *The Social Contract* (1762), probably the most influential and outstanding work of political philosophy of the 18th century. It was a natural successor to his earlier work, *The Discourse on Inequality* (1755), in which he criticized the injustice he witnessed everywhere in the world around him. He saw this as the direct result of educational and social structures that suppressed the natural will and ability of men.

JEAN-JACQUES ROUSSEAU (1712–78)
The son of a watchmaker, Jean-Jacques Rousseau was born in Geneva, Switzerland. His mother died in childbirth and his father abandoned him when he fled Geneva to escape

impending legal difficulties. Rousseau himself left Geneva at the age of 15. In 1728 he was employed as a steward by a 29-year-old noblewoman, Françoise-Louise de Warens, who was being paid by the king of Piedmont to convert Protestants to Catholicism. Following his own conversion, Rousseau worked as a servant, secretary and tutor, travelling through France and Italy. De Warens introduced him to the world of letters and ideas, and finally took him as her lover when he was 20 years old. He regarded her as the love of his life.

At the age of 27, Rousseau moved to Lyon to work as a tutor; then, in 1742, he moved to Paris, where he met Denis Diderot. The two men became the focal point for a group of radical intellectuals, though Rousseau's belief in the natural goodness of humanity set him apart from the others. He published his first important work, A Discourse on the Sciences and the Arts, *in 1750, then went on to publish* Discourse on the Origin of Inequality *in 1755. In* The Social Contract *of 1762 he recommended how man might recover his natural freedom in exchange for obedience to a self-imposed law.*

Tiring of Paris, he left for Montmorency where he wrote Èmile, *a treatise on education, and* The New Eloise,

a novel which scandalized the French authorities who burned it and ordered the author's arrest. After spending time in England, Rousseau returned to France and wrote Confessions, *justifying his philosophy against his opponents. He died in 1778.*

In the famous opening line of *The Social Contract* (see quote below) Rousseau set out his premise that society robs humankind of nobility and natural freedom. However, he goes on to say that it is the social contract – the covenant between individuals agreeing to be governed – which renders us free. The freedom the solitary human enjoys is the freedom to pursue personal well-being without comparison or harmful consideration of others. Society, with its trappings of wealth and ambition, removes this freedom. We become concerned with what others possess, with our position in relation to others, and thus become dissatisfied, acquisitive, envious and cruel. Instead of a natural impulse to attain the essentials we need – food, shelter, a mate – we strive for unnecessary things that society has taught us to desire. This has come about because the societies we have built (and it holds true today, as well as in 18th-century France) have a faulty social contract. People have been coerced into giving up their natural freedoms in exchange for a form of slavery in a society designed by and for the rich.

> '*Man was born free, and he is everywhere in chains. Those who think themselves the masters of others are indeed greater slaves than they.*'
>
> Jean-Jacques Rousseau, *The Social Contract* (1762)

A good society, according to Rousseau, is based on principles of classical republicanism. The people come together and govern in a democracy that sets laws for the benefit of society as a whole. As the laws are an expression of general will, it is in each person's interests to obey them; to do so is both an expression and attainment of freedom.

> 'The first man who, having fenced in a piece of land, said, "This is mine," and found people naïve enough to believe him, that man was the true founder of civil society. From how many crimes, wars, and murders, from how many horrors and misfortunes might not any one have saved mankind, by pulling up the stakes, or filling up the ditch, and crying to his fellows: Beware of listening to this impostor; you are undone if you once forget that the fruits of the earth belong to us all, and the earth itself to nobody.'
>
> Jean-Jacques Rousseau,
> *Discourse on the Origin of Inequality* (1755)

Rousseau even goes so far as to say that any notion of individual rights must be given up, as they should not be necessary in the properly constituted society because what is good-for-all is necessarily good-for-one. This all looks hopelessly optimistic, and there are of course many cases in which what is good for the many does not look at all good for every individual. Rousseau recognized that people don't necessarily know what is good for them, and explained that when they don't know their 'real will' they need a great legislator to reveal it to them.

TRUSTING THE GENERAL WILL

More than just the sum of all the individual wills, the general will is directed towards the communal good:

> 'Each of us puts his person and all his power in common under the supreme direction of the general will, and, in our corporate capacity, we receive each member as an indivisible part of the whole.'

By exercising the general will, we avoid the exploitation or neglect of minority groups. For example, it would benefit the majority of people in a country where most people are not red-headed to confiscate the goods of red-headed people and redistribute them among people who do not have red hair. This would prioritize the majority will (the will of the majority of individuals) over the general will. The will of the individuals who make up society is to enhance their personal wealth. But the general will works to create an equitable and sustainable society with minimal conflict and injustice. So, while the majority will may be served by confiscating and redistributing the property of red-headed people, the general will is served by allowing red-headed people to own property on the same terms as everyone else.

Rousseau regarded the ruler as the agent, not the master, of the people. His assertion that everyone should follow what is deemed to be the general good, as set out by the ruler, caused some to accuse him of licensing totalitarianism and tyranny. But he argued that as the sovereign can only impose rules in the name of the general will, he or she cannot become a despot because there is no disjunction between what the sovereign ordains and the interests of the people.

Rousseau insisted that his social plan would only really succeed in small city-states, such as those of Ancient Greece. This is a distinct problem for a world comprising large nation-states and even empires. At the end of *The Social Contract*, Rousseau asks, 'What is to be done?' His answer is that everyone must cultivate their own personal virtues and obey the rule of law.

Revolution!

The French people gave a different answer to Rousseau's philosophical question. Their response was one feared by governments throughout Europe – the overthrow of the rule of law. One of the important questions in political philosophy is under what

In the 19th century, staunch Conservatives resisted calls for social reform because they believed that wrongs would naturally right themselves with time. This non-interventionist approach to social problems came at a great human cost.

circumstances can a ruler legitimately be overthrown? Aristotle made the point that a tyrant is not acting like a ruler and therefore surrenders the right to rule. This view was taken up by Aquinas and carried on into the Middle Ages. Machiavelli focused on helping the ruler to stay on the right side of tyranny to ensure that the people would not revolt. The true philosophers of revolt, however, came to the fore in the 18th century – and revolutions followed.

THE FRENCH REVOLUTION

The French Revolution was the bloodiest collective uprising of the 18th and 19th centuries. It was fuelled by the people's fury at the extravagant lifestyles of the aristocracy, fiscal problems in France, and by Enlightenment ideas about equality and freedom. In 1789, the starving peasantry and urban poor rose up against the ruling classes and revolution ensued, beginning with the storming of the Bastille prison in Paris. In 1792, a republic was declared and King Louis XVI was executed the following year.

Struggles and dissent between the revolutionaries marked the whole period. Between 1793 and 1794, Maximilien Robespierre, leader of the Jacobins, headed a 'Reign of Terror' in which up to 40,000 people including nobles and priests were killed, many executed by guillotine. The Jacobins fell in 1795 and a bourgeois republic (the Directory) took control of France until it was abolished by a new leader, Napoleon Bonaparte, in 1799.

COMMON-SENSE MORALITY?

In 1774, the English-born political philosopher Thomas Paine (1737–1809) emigrated to America, where he wrote for and later edited the *Pennsylvania Magazine* and published one of the first essays calling for the abolition of slavery. At the start of the American War of Independence in 1776, Paine anonymously published a pamphlet titled *Common Sense* in support of the revolution. It recommended that America throw off its British colonial overlords and become self-governing. As well as detailing Paine's objections to a constitutional monarchy, the pamphlet proposed a method of democratic government. Paine argued against any hereditary office or aristocracy, and said that government and social status should be kept separate. He claimed that independence for the American colonies was justified morally and practically, as they could be self-supporting.

After the War of Independence, Paine went first to France and then to England. Responding to Edmund Burke's *Reflections*

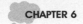

on the Revolution in France (1790), Paine produced his seminal treatise on democracy, *The Rights of Man*, in 1791. In this he asserted that all men are born with equal rights, but living socially means that we can't always defend our rights or avoid violating the rights of others. By establishing a state and a constitution, we can encode our rights as civil rights that can be defended and enforced on our behalf. In Paine's view, the only morally acceptable form of government is a democratic republic in which citizens vote to choose their leaders. England and France, he claimed, had immoral constitutions as citizens were denied this right. This, according to Paine, was sufficient justification for the populations of England and France to overthrow their governments.

> *'A statue of gold should be erected to you in every city in the universe.'*
>
> Emperor Napoleon Bonaparte of France,
> talking to Thomas Paine
>
> *'The completest charlatan that ever existed.'*
>
> Thomas Paine, commenting on
> Emperor Napoleon Bonaparte

The British government immediately charged Paine with treason and, once he had fled to France, quashed the incipient British revolution. Paine was welcomed in France and given a seat at the National Convention, but the country was still in a volatile state and he was later imprisoned on Robespierre's orders. He escaped execution only because of Robespierre's own downfall. Paine returned to America in 1802, but his rejection of organized religion and of the idea of a vengeful God made him deeply unpopular, and he died in obscurity.

EDMUND BURKE, *REFLECTIONS ON THE REVOLUTION IN FRANCE* (1790)

The Irish statesman and philosopher Edmund Burke (1729–97) declared that the French Revolution would fail disastrously as its guiding principles took no account of human nature. He spoke against Enlightenment and the ideas of Hobbes, saying that society should be handled like a living organism – infinitely complex and requiring compassionate engagement – and not be reduced to a set of rules. He promoted slow, constitutional change to introduce specific rights and liberties rather than radical overthrow by means of a revolution in the name of abstract Rights and Liberty. With considerable prescience, Burke predicted that the revolution in France would lead to squabbling factions until eventually one general would emerge as leader and start to edge towards tyranny.

THE 'HYENA IN PETTICOATS'

Thinking along the same lines as Thomas Paine, Mary Wollstonecraft (1759–97) was one of the few influential female philosophers to have lived before the 20th century. Now famous for her *Vindication of the Rights of Woman* (1792), a text that arguably initiated the feminist movement, she was a political philosopher of considerable talent. But Wollstonecraft wrote first about the rights of men.

Responding to Burke's *Reflections on the French Revolution*, her *Vindication of the Rights of Men* (published anonymously) argued that the people should have the right to remove a bad king, and that slavery and contemporary treatment of the poor were immoral. She called for the dissolution of the monarchy and an end to the power of the Church, both of which she considered oppressive.

But it was her *Vindication of the Rights of Woman*, published with her name on the title page, that caused fur to fly. The American stateman Aaron Burr declared it 'a work of genius', while the English writer Horace Walpole branded its author a 'hyena in petticoats'. In her masterwork, Wollstonecraft suggests that women 'labour by reforming themselves to reform the world'. She saw education as the focus for reform. The educational practices of the time, she said, did not equip women to participate as citizens and make use of their abilities, but only served to make them decorative servants to men. She wrote: 'The minds of women are enfeebled by false refinement,' deploring the way in which both sexes focus only on how women look. She argued that by this route women were encouraged to be docile and to enter into marriages that were effectively 'legal prostitution':

Mary Wollstonecraft was the first significant female philosopher of the modern era.

'I have turned over various books written on the subject of education, and patiently observed the conduct of parents and the management of schools; but what has been the result? A profound conviction that the neglected education of my fellow-creatures is the grand source of the misery I deplore.'

Her insistence that women should take responsibility for shaping their own characters is as arresting today as it was in the 18th century:

'The first object of laudable ambition is to obtain a character as a human being.'

Wollstonecraft was adamant that the subjugation of women is harmful to men as well, as it reduces the portion of reason, knowledge and virtue available to benefit society as a whole. Bad treatment of women, she argued, encourages them to be sly, debases them, creates discord in the home and perpetuates the wrong values because they pass the same behaviour on to their children.

'The civilized women of the present century, with a few exceptions, are only anxious to inspire love, when they ought to cherish a nobler ambition, and by their abilities and virtues exact respect.'

Mary Wollstonecraft, *Vindication of the Rights of Woman* (1792)

Had Wollstonecraft not died at the age of 38, just ten days after giving birth to her daughter, feminist philosophy might have progressed a lot more quickly than it did. The daughter, Mary Wollstonecraft Shelley, survived and went on to write the celebrated Gothic novel, *Frankenstein* (1823).

THE SPIRIT OF THE LAWS

In 1748, the French political philosopher Charles de Secondat, Baron de Montesquieu, analyzed political structures and isolated three of them, each driven by a spirit or 'spring':

- *For democratic and aristocratic republics, the spring is the love of virtue – the willingness to put the interests of the community ahead of private interests. An aristocratic republic is one in which power is restricted to a few, such as the noble families who were allowed a vote in the Venetian Republic. A democratic republic allows everyone – or at least every male – a vote.*
- *For monarchies, the spring is the love of honour – the drive for rank and privilege.*
- *For despotic regimes, the spring is fear.*

If the spring is not powerful enough to sustain the social order, the political system will collapse. Montesquieu said that the English did not manage to retain a republic under Oliver Cromwell because they had an insufficient love of virtue.

Social mathematics

Despite Burke's plea for a compassionate, heart-based government, the end of the 18th century saw a move towards an almost mechanically mathematical approach to society and law-building. The seminal capitalist text and the development of utilitarianism both belong to this period.

THE MATHS OF MONEY

At exactly the same time that Paine was stirring up revolution with his pamphlet *Common Sense*, the Scottish moral philosopher Adam Smith (1723–90) was taking the opposite view by explaining and justifying the inequalities in the political system. Known now as the economic theorist favoured by British prime minister Margaret Thatcher, Smith published his treatise on capitalism, *An Inquiry into the Nature and Causes of the Wealth of Nations*, in 1776.

Adam Smith firmly believed that the 'unintended consequences of intended action' benefit society. By this he meant that in serving their own interests, people would unintentionally serve the interests of society as a whole. For example, suppose a man decides to set up a business selling vegetables door to door. He does this because he wants to make a living and be his own boss. But there are unintentional benefits for other people: customers no longer have to make their way to the shops or market; farmers benefit because he buys their produce; and he provides jobs in the community when his business expands and he employs other people. Smith promoted a free-market economy, where these unintentional benefits only occur if a door-to-door vegetable service is genuinely good for the local community. If too few people want this service, his business won't succeed or he will have to adapt it to suit the market conditions.

The problem with this model is that people are only going to consume a finite amount of vegetables. If they are buying from the door-to-door salesman, they are not buying from someone else, so other vegetable-sellers suffer as a result of the competition.

Smith's free-market philosophy was played out in the 'unintended consequences' of extreme poverty and deprivation, exploitative working practices and a life of misery and degradation for the working-class poor of the Industrial Revolution.

Smith's philosophy does not provide for the exploited losers in the free market – losers who were once in Western factories and farms or on the slave plantations of the American South, but are now in the factories of emergent economic powers and on the farms of South America, Africa and Asia. Nevertheless, *The Wealth of Nations* remains one of the most important and influential works of economic and political philosophy in the history of Western thought.

UTILITY AND UTILITARIANISM

The belief that the 'unintended consequences of intended action' will benefit society influenced the industrial philanthropists of the 18th and 19th centuries, and also had a bearing on the ideas of philosophers such as Jeremy Bentham. Bentham developed the principle of 'utility' – the idea that humankind is motivated by the desire to seek pleasure and avoid pain. He applied this to political science, drawing up plans for a society and a legal code based on delivering the greatest good (pleasure) to the greatest number of people. In *Introduction to the Principles of Morals and Legislation* (1789), the first document to outline utilitarianism, Bentham explained that legislation should try to harmonize the interests of society with those of private individuals pursuing their own happiness.

> 'Nature has placed mankind under the governance of two sovereign masters, pain and pleasure. . . . They govern us in all we do, in all we say, in all we think: every effort we can make to throw off our subjection will serve but to demonstrate and confirm it. In words a man may pretend to abjure their empire, but in reality he will remain subject to it all the while.'
>
> Jeremy Bentham, *An Introduction to the Principles of Morals and Legislation* (1789)

> 'The business of government is to promote the happiness of the society, by punishing and rewarding. . . . In proportion as an act tends to disturb that happiness, in proportion as the tendency of it is pernicious, will be the demand it creates for punishment.'
>
> Jeremy Bentham, *An Introduction to the Principles of Morals and Legislation* (1789)

Bentham was a great reformer and campaigned for many liberal causes. These included the abolition of slavery and all forms of corporal punishment, the promotion of social equality for women, the decriminalization of consensual homosexuality, and an end to animal cruelty. Some of these ideas were too pioneering for his time – his essay on homosexuality was not published until 1931.

Most famously, Bentham designed an institutional building called a 'panopticon', in which prisoners would be visible to their guardians at all times (see panel below). His theory was that being on view would encourage the prisoners to behave well and therefore promote the greatest good for the greatest number; if the prisoners behaved obediently, they would not be punished and would not have to endure pain. The intention was to reform the criminals; the extent of their punishment was carefully calculated so that its long-term consequences would be a net increase in pleasure.

BENTHAM'S PANOPTICON

Bentham's design for a prison consisted of a ring of cells on several tiers arranged around a central watch-tower. The cells have glass fronts. The occupant of the watch-tower can see into all the cells, but the inmate of a cell can't see into the watch-tower. The French philosopher Michel Foucault described it as

'a machine for dissociating the "see/being seen" dyad: in the peripheric ring, one is totally seen, without ever seeing; in the central tower, one sees everything without ever being seen.'

Bentham designed it on the principle that surveillance should be 'visible and unverifiable'. The prisoners are aware

> *that they could be watched at all times, but do not know*
> *when they are actually being watched. The effect is the same*
> *as if they were being watched all the time, as the prisoners*
> *become self-regulating in their behaviour.*

Putting morality on a practical and quantitative footing, Bentham even devised an algorithm for calculating whether or not a proposed action or rule is good. He called it the 'felicific calculus', and it involves a classification of 12 pains and 14 pleasures. He described it in his *Introduction to the Principles of Morals and Legislation*. For each action, we need to consider the pleasures and pains that will result from it, taking account of their intensity, duration, certainty, propinquity (how soon the pleasure or pain will occur), fecundity (the chance that the sensation will be followed by more of the same kind), purity (the chance that the sensation will be followed by the opposite type), and extent (how many people are affected). Bentham wanted the calculator to be used in reforming criminal law. Using the calculator, it should have been possible to work out the minimum penalty to act as a deterrent to prevent any specific crime.

TROUBLE AT T'MILL

Bentham makes no distinction between happiness and pleasure, and treats pleasures and pain like countable beans that are directly and quantitatively comparable – views with which his successor, John Stuart Mill, took issue. Like Rousseau, Bentham subordinated the good of the individual to the good of society in a way that, logically extended, could lead to the sacrifice of the one for the good of the many. It was a problem which Mill did not resolve in his subsequent development of utilitarianism.

Mill's 'greatest happiness' principle:
'Actions are right in proportion as they tend to promote happiness, wrong as they tend to produce the reverse of happiness. By happiness is intended pleasure, and the absence of pain; by unhappiness, pain, and the privation of pleasure.'

Mill agreed with Bentham that moral action should maximize pleasure and minimize pain and that this goal could guide us in choosing how to act. But he said that pleasure can't be reduced to a mere quantitative analysis without taking qualitative aspects into account. Not all pains and pleasures are equal – the pain of losing a pet is not the same as that of losing a parent – and even the way pain and pleasure are 'rated' varies between individuals. Bentham's happiness calculator could not properly take account of these distinctions. Mill also insisted that some pleasures are of greater value than others. He felt that it was necessary to distinguish between 'higher' and 'lower' pleasures in the utilitarian calculation.

Mill's radical liberal view deemed that it was not necessary for us to scrutinize every action of daily life and choose the option that created the greatest happiness for the largest number. He maintained that only when there are points of moral choice do we need to use that method. He stood up for the rights of the individual against the state, and spoke out for personal freedoms. In *On Liberty* (1859), he argued that:

'The only purpose for which power can be rightfully exercised over any member of a civilized community, against his will, is to prevent harm to others.'

MODERN UTILITARIANS

The Australian moral philosopher Peter Singer (born 1946) is a modern-day utilitarian, promoting what he calls 'preference utilitarianism'. While classical utilitarianism compares the morality of choice of actions by calculating which brings the greatest happiness to the most people, Singer decides the morality of an action by how far it satisfies desires and preferences. In making a judgement, we must look at the interests of all those involved and affected and choose the course that satisfies the most and frustrates the fewest desires and preferences. This all sounds fair enough, but Singer takes his argument to lengths that many consider extreme.

For Singer, we need to take account of quality of life, including a person's capacity to experience pleasure and self-fulfilment and to avoid suffering. In some cases, the conclusion might be that some lives are not worth living. He endorses suicide, abortion, voluntary euthanasia and even involuntary euthanasia where the subject is unable to decide their own fate for physical reasons. He argues that seriously disabled infants could be killed up to the age of 28 days, as newborns lack the essential characteristics of personhood – 'rationality, autonomy and self-consciousness'. He would condone such killings if they were in the best interests of the afflicted individual and/or the family.

At the same time, Singer considers it morally indefensible that the rights afforded to humans should not also be afforded to animals, which are sentient beings capable of suffering pain. He rejects all cruelty to animals, including factory farming and animal experimentation, as manifestations of 'speciesism' comparable with racism and sexism.

This is not because animals are inherently 'equal' to humans (any more than all humans are equal in terms of their individual attributes), but that animals must be given equal consideration.

Singer's preference for utilitarianism could also be applied to the ethics of wealth distribution. He starts with the assumption that 'suffering and death from lack of food, shelter and medical care are bad', and argues that if we can prevent suffering and death in one place, without causing greater harm elsewhere, then we should do so. He uses the analogy of seeing a child drowning in a pond. If we saw a drowning child, we would rush into the pond to save the child, even at the expense of ruining our clothes and shoes: the loss of the clothes and shoes is a far lesser evil than the death of a child. The distance between ourselves and the sufferer is of no relevance, so if we are ever in a position to alleviate suffering, we should do so. It follows that if we were prepared to lose a pair of shoes to save a child drowning in a pond in front of us, then 'if for the cost of a pair of shoes we can contribute to a health program in a developing country that stands a good chance of saving the life of a child, we ought to do so.'

> 'If possessing a higher degree of intelligence does not entitle one human to use another for his own ends, how can it entitle humans to exploit nonhumans?'
> Peter Singer, *Animal Rights and Human Obligations* (1989)

Peter Singer's book Animal Liberation *(1975) argues that cruelty to animals is morally unjustifiable.*

Towards communism

While philosophers of diverse political beliefs commented on the French and American revolutions, two German philosophers and social theorists would have a profound impact on 19th-century politics. Karl Marx and Friedrich Engels have probably done more to shape the world than any other political thinkers, for their writings were not simply debated but taken up by revolutionaries and put into action.

MARX AND ENGELS

Marx and Engels worked closely with each other and are often spoken of in the same breath. Karl Marx is famous for his great work *Capital: Critique of Political Economy* (1867–93), better known as *Das Kapital*. Friedrich Engels wrote the highly influential *The Condition of the Working Class in England* (1845). Together they wrote *The Communist Manifesto* (1848). The philosophy underpinning their works is rooted in the ideas of Georg Hegel, who provided the notion of 'dialectic' – an approach to truth through the proposition of theses, each of which is opposed by antitheses, eventually leading to a synthesis which then becomes the new thesis. Whereas Hegel's dialectic was directed towards an absolute truth bound up in the divine, Marx and Engels favoured a 'dialectical materialism' which had no recourse to God and dealt not with ideas but with actualities. This sounds more complex than it is: Marx and Engels simply meant that a repeating pattern of conflicts (in the form of class struggle) will lead inevitably to the 'correct' social structure.

> '*The philosophers have only interpreted the world, the point is to change it.*'
>
> Karl Marx, *Theses on Feuerbach* (1845)

Karl Marx was born in Prussia in 1818 and moved to Paris in 1843; he was exiled from this city in 1849 and spent the rest of his life in London.

For Marx and Engels, the fundamental condition of humanity is the need to convert the raw material of the natural world into the goods necessary for survival. For example, to dig metal from the ground and turn it into spoons and other useful objects. As a result, the means of production, or the control of it, determines the shape of society:

'The hand-mill gives a society with the feudal lord; the steam-mill a society with the industrial capitalist.'

THE CONDITION OF THE WORKING CLASS IN ENGLAND (1845)

The Russian communist revolutionary Vladimir Lenin (1874–1920) described Friedrich Engels' book The Condition of the Working Class in England *as 'a terrible indictment of capitalism and the bourgeoisie . . . filled with the most authentic and shocking pictures of the misery of the English proletariat'. In this treatise, Engels writes:*

'What security has the working-man that it may not be his turn tomorrow? Who assures him employment, who vouches for it that, if for any reason or no reason his lord and master discharges him tomorrow, he can struggle along with those dependent upon him, until he may find someone else "to give him bread"? Who guarantees that willingness to work shall suffice to obtain work, that uprightness, industry, thrift, and the rest of the virtues recommended by the bourgeoisie, are really his road to happiness? No one. He knows that he has something today and that it does not depend upon himself whether he shall have something tomorrow.'

Marx and Engels believed that political history was based on a pattern of permanent opposition in the form of class struggle, with one social structure replacing another in turn. The land-owners created by feudalism were being opposed by a rising mercantile middle class, who formed a new economic class of capitalist industrialists. The new thesis of capitalism was then challenged by the disenchanted working classes (the proletariat). The inevitable outcome of this, said Marx and Engels, was communism. The argument for communism was not based on ethical judgements. Rather, communism was the most efficient means of providing the goods needed for survival and therefore was the natural outcome of economic conditions.

While Hegel saw changes in ideology and human under-standing as the drivers of social and political change, Marx and Engels saw economic and social change leading to new ways of thinking. Marx did not see the human mind as a passive subject

During the Russian Revolution of 1917, the tsar's autocratic government was overthrown following an uprising by the workers.

in an external world. He shared Kant's view that the mind is actively engaged with the objects of knowledge. But he went further than Kant, suggesting that both the mind and the world are continually adapting, and that we order our experience in ways that make it useful to our survival.

For this reason, Marx didn't believe social structures could be reformed from the top down. In his view, society can only truly change from the bottom up – when the workers become aware of the oppressive situation they are in and rebel against it. Once society had changed, then thinking would also change. Consequently, Marx didn't feel it was possible to predict the form that communism would take – this could only be discovered after a social and economic revolution had occurred.

Unlike many of their contemporaries, Marx and Engels did not deplore the existence of the proletariat; they believed the larger the proletariat, the sooner the revolution would come.

The deplorable conditions that working people were enduring would make them realize that change was necessary. Revolutions occurred both in Russia and China during the 20th century, with disastrous consequences and leading to the deaths of millions of people – which is something neither Marx nor Engels is likely to have foreseen.

COUNTER-COMMUNISM

The world over, ruling capitalists obviously disliked the idea that their workers could rise up and overthrow them. The work of the British economist John Maynard Keynes (1883–1946) seemed to offer a way of avoiding this. According to Keynesian economics, a downturn in the economy is a short-term problem resulting from a lack of demand. It can be solved by government increasing public spending to boost demand. Intervention by government could lead to a stable free-market economy that would prevent the collapse of capitalism and the subsequent emergence of communism. This is the opposite of the approach advocated by Smith and Mill, who believed that if allowed to take its natural

John Maynard Keynes recommended increased government spending as the way to lead an economy out of recession.

course the economic order would move towards the maximum well-being for the individual and for society as a whole.

REVOLUTION TAKEN TO EXTREMES

It is difficult to find a social and political structure that is fair and workable to all. Some philosophers have considered it impossible and in preference would do away with all structures. The Russian revolutionary and thinker Mikhail Bakunin was the first true anarchist philosopher. He called for the overthrow of all styles of external authority, from God downwards, saying that people should be entirely self-governing.

> 'The liberty of man consists solely in this, that he obeys the laws of nature because he has himself recognized them as such, and not because they have been imposed upon him externally by any foreign will whatsoever, human or divine, collective or individual.'
>
> Mikhail Bakunin, *God and the State* (1871)

Bakunin developed a form of socialism called collective anarchism, whereby the people would take possession of and manage the means of production, the land and everything else. They would have freedom of association and federation. Everyone, male and female, would have equal opportunities for education and equal means of subsistence and support. The peasants would 'take the land and throw out those landlords who live by the labour of others'. Unlike Marx, Bakunin did not exclude the *Lumpenproletariat* (which roughly translates as 'slum workers' or 'mob') from his scheme – rather, the success of his project depended upon them, as they had the least attachment to the bourgeois model.

LUMPENPROLETARIAT

Marx defines the Lumpenproletariat *as the lowest class of the masses. It includes those who refuse to work and those who can't work through reasons of sickness and disability:*

'*Vagabonds, discharged soldiers, discharged jailbirds, escaped galley slaves, swindlers, mountebanks, lazzaroni [street people], pickpockets, tricksters, gamblers, maquereaux [pimps], brothel keepers, porters, literati, organ grinders, ragpickers, knife grinders, tinkers, beggars — in short, the whole indefinite, disintegrated mass.*'

Karl Marx, *The Eighteenth Brumaire of Louis Napoleon* (1852)

With some prescience, Bakunin saw that Marxism was not going to go well if implemented. Although he and Marx shared the same goal, Bakunin envisaged it being achieved by the proletariat rising up under their own steam and overthrowing all imposed social structures. Marx, on the other hand, wanted to act on behalf of the proletariat, creating a state that would, in theory, put their interests first. Bakunin objected:

'*In reality, this would be for the proletariat a barrack-regime, under which the workingmen and the working-women, converted into a uniform mass, would rise, fall asleep, work, and live at the beat of the drum.*'

ALL TOTALITARIAN IN THE END

The communist revolution ultimately led to the totalitarian state, which gave its workers no more freedom than did the dictatorship, its polar opposite. In both cases, the state as an entity in its own right took precedence over the individuals which comprised it. It is against this backdrop of a world ravaged by the failure of totalitarianism that the philosophers of the second half of the 20th century tried to piece together a more humane relationship between the state and the individual.

The American cognitive scientist and philosopher Noam Chomsky (born 1928) considers that humans can only endure certain types of political structure. He believes that a certain degree of free-ness (the desire to be free to choose our actions and mode of life) is an innate feature of the human mind. Any political structure which tries to deny this or crush the individual is ultimately doomed to failure.

> *'He called me a sentimental idealist and he was right; I called him a vain man, perfidious and crafty, and I also was right.'*
>
> Mikhail Bakunin on meeting Karl Marx (1844)

'No such thing as society'

In 1987, British prime minister Margaret Thatcher declared, 'there is no such thing as society'. Her words were an extreme extrapolation of the political philosophy of the American philosopher Robert Nozick (1938–2002). In 1974, Nozick argued for individual rights, following Kant's dictum:

> *'Act so that you treat humanity, whether in your own person or in that of another, always as an end and never as a means only.'*

> ### LIBERTARIANISM
> *Libertarianism generally applies to a belief in the innate freedom of individuals and the reduction or removal of the state. Anarchism is extreme libertarianism.*

Nozick's version involved a full-blown libertarian dismantling of the authority of social structures. In *Anarchy, State and Utopia* (1974), he argues that all individuals are 'self-owners', so all individual rights – over mind, body, abilities or goods – must be considered as property rights. These rights are absolute and can't be overridden by the state or any other collective authority.

Angry protests against public spending cuts are frequently witnessed in a democratically governed state. A libertarian model would see public spending in the hands of private enterprise, and possibly even angrier protests as a result.

According to Nozick, a welfare state that takes money in taxes is indulging in institutionalized theft, and progressive taxation is a form of 'forced labour'. Even if the state is democratically sanctioned, it is a violation of the individual's rights to take their time, money or labour. He proposed a minimalist 'night-watchman' state, which protected its citizens from violence and enforced laws governing the fair acquisition and transfer of property. Other functions often taken on by the state, such as education, healthcare and welfare, should be left to private businesses and charities.

Socio-economic development would be driven by the free market, unregulated by rent controls or minimum wage agreements, both of which violate the rights of the individual. Instead of distributive justice, Nozick preferred 'entitlement justice' – there would be no state assets to distribute, and an individual would be entitled to anything justly acquired. The 'justness' of acquisition was defined by a complex set of rules governing acquisition and transfers.

ALL'S FAIR IN LOVE AND . . . BASKETBALL
Nozick illustrated the concept of entitlement justice using the example of a famous American basketball champion, Wilt Chamberlain.

Let's assume that everyone in the USA starts with an equal amount of money which they can choose to spend as they wish. Chamberlain says he will only play basketball if each member of the audience pays 25 cents to him each time he plays. At the end of the season, a million people have paid to see him play, so he has $250,000. Chamberlain is now much richer than everyone else. But he is entitled to the money

> *as each person paid freely, in full knowledge of the situation, and everyone who didn't pay kept their 25 cents. What can be the excuse for taking away some of Chamberlain's money and redistributing it? If the first distribution was fair, when everyone was given the same amount of money, surely the new distribution of wealth is too?*

During the 1980s, some aspects of Nozick's political philosophy found favour with right-wing politicians. The anti-foundationalist Richard Rorty advocated reducing the state's role to a minimum which simply protects people from cruelty or extreme poverty. He saw that there were, in practical terms, limits to how far anti-foundationalist politics could be implemented and hoped that with imagination and creativity, people would be able to 'describ[e] a future in terms which the past did not use'.

INTO THE FUTURE

Over a century ago, Friedrich Nietzsche observed that the strong come to dominate in society: he described these as the 'self-realized', those who can control their passions and channel the 'will to power' into a creative force. Nietzsche said that the 'self-realized' have a moral duty to help the less virtuous.

> *'The man of virtue, too, helps the unfortunate, but not, or almost not, out of pity, but prompted by an urge which is begotten by the excess of power.'*
> Friedrich Nietzsche, *Beyond Good and Evil* (1886)

There is a long tradition of philanthropy among the very wealthy, with some of the most successful people giving away large sums of money to support the arts, medical research or education in their own communities and elsewhere in the world. But, in general, a minimalist state has not worked. The good will of a few individuals is not sufficient to bolster the whole of society, and the gap between rich and poor is growing ever wider.

Society and sociology

The French philosopher Auguste Comte (1798–1857) was the first to apply the methods of science to the study of people and societies. His work was based on the 'statics and dynamics' of society and led to the modern discipline of sociology.

SHAKY BEGINNINGS

From statics (the science of forces in equilibrium), Comte concluded that no part of the 'social consensus' can be changed without affecting the whole: economic, cultural and social conditions are all connected. From dynamics (the science of change), he decided that the development of society mirrors the development of intellectual progress. Social orders had moved through stages of theocracy, monarchy and anarchy, and the next phase would be a new social order led by science.

PERSONAL AND PUBLIC CONSCIENCE

The French sociologist Émile Durkheim (1858–1917) undertook to show how all human societies are bound together and organized by moral rules. In *The Division of Labour in Society* (1893), he carried out a historical investigation which examined how moral rules have operated in societies. Like Comte, Durkheim felt the need for a kind of 'science of morality' to make this possible, and used scientific methodology to analyze social structures. He found that as societies evolve from what he called a 'primitive' to a 'modern' state, there is a move from collective to individual conscience and moral rules. Traditional societies tend to be devoutly religious and most people in them share the same moral values based on their shared faith. Any violation of the rules tends to be strongly condemned and punished severely. As societies evolve, the hold of these religious beliefs weakens, morality diverges and tolerance increases.

But instead of seeing this as the fragmentation of collective conscience, Durkheim saw it as another expression of it: the collective conscience tolerating individuation, the process whereby individuals develop a variety of beliefs independent of any dominant moral authority. What emerges is 'the cult of the individual' – a new moral code that emphasizes the right of individuals to develop in accordance with their own beliefs.

The surprising conclusion is that, according to Durkheim's argument, individualism does not reflect an erosion of old moral values in society, but an expression of new ones. Modern societies have diverse economic relations based on diverse beliefs and values, and the 'cult of the individual' is a new moral code reflecting a new social and economic order.

> 'In the same way as the ideal of the less developed societies was to create or maintain as intense a shared life as possible, in which the individual was absorbed, our ideal is constantly to introduce greater equality in our social relations, in order to ensure the free unfolding of socially useful forces.'
> Émile Durkheim, *The Division of Labour in Society* (1893)

CHAPTER 6

Justice as fairness

Since Plato, political philosophers have looked to design an egalitarian political and judicial system, or one that they believe will evolve naturally. The American political philosopher John Rawls (1921–2002) suggested a beautifully simple method for designing a fair society. His 'Justice as Fairness' theory updates the social contract, protecting individual rights and promoting distributive justice at the same time. He starts from what he calls the 'original position'. This requires that people work from behind a 'veil of ignorance' to decide what is fair. They have to construct their judicial and social systems without knowing what position they, as individuals, will occupy in society. They have to consider whether they will be the most menial worker or a member of the ruling class. In this situation they are bound to adopt what Rawls called a 'maximin strategy' – a self-protecting set of principles that is fair for everyone. These are:

'The principles that rational and free persons concerned to further their own interests would accept in an initial position of equality as defining the fundamentals of the terms of their association.'

Rawls believed that people would come up with two Principles of Justice. The First (Liberty) Principle states that 'each person is to have an equal right to the most extensive scheme of equal basic liberties compatible with a similar scheme of liberty for others'. These basic liberties include freedom of speech, assembly, thought and conscience, and the right to hold personal property. They do not include the classic 'freedoms from', such as freedom from unemployment, exploitation or fear.

The Second (Justice) Principle is in two parts. First, everyone must have equality of opportunity in terms of gaining jobs or positions of power, and this entails equality of educational provision. Second, inequality is only acceptable if it raises the absolute level of the worst-off. No one should expect greater rewards simply because they were lucky enough to be born with greater gifts.

Rawls recognized that the two principles could work against each other, so he made the Liberty Principle more or less absolute – it must take precedence, except in situations of low economic development. He refused an international application of the 'Difference Principle', claiming that countries, unlike individuals, had no right to expect compensation for a lack of natural resources.

FIVE POLITICAL SYSTEMS

In 1971, Rawls assessed the following five political systems with reference to his Principles of Justice and Liberty:

- *Laissez-faire capitalism*
- *State socialism with a command economy*
- *Welfare-state capitalism*
- *Property-owning democracy*
- *Market socialism*

Initially Rawls thought only the first two unworkable, but by 2001 his experience of social problems in the USA during the 1980s and 1990s had led him to reject welfare-state capitalism as well. Only a property-owning democracy or market socialism remain as viable, according to Rawls.

The applications of philosophy

—

'The point of philosophy is to start with
something so simple as not to seem worth
stating, and to end with something so
paradoxical that no one will believe it.'
Bertrand Russell,
The Philosophy of Logical Atomism (1918)

'I feel that we are all philosophers, and that those who describe themselves as a philosopher simply do not have a day job to go to.'
Kevin Warwick, British engineer (quoted 2004)

The fabric of philosophy

For the Algerian-born French post-structuralist philosopher Jacques Derrida, the meanings of words are fluid and subjective. For every individual, a word or utterance has meaning that is garnered from personal history and experience, from connotations not known by or accessible to the original speaker. The network of associations for a word extends through personal and public space and time. The lack of objective meaning has particular impact when we discuss metaphysical concepts such as 'self' and 'virtue'. A word such as 'self' necessarily implies its opposite, 'other'. Derrida claims that the concept of 'self' is a linguistic construction with no metaphysical or ontological necessity. Of course, a philosopher dismantling language is sawing through the branch he is sitting on. He has nothing to offer in place of language and no way of justifying his authority, as he has discredited the medium by which it is conveyed.

Philosophy is a subject where it is difficult to arrive at 'correct' answers. While the questions in other disciplines can often be answered with empirical evidence – DNA is the means of biological inheritance, for example, or earthquakes are caused by the movement of tectonic plates – such a framework seldom applies to philosophical questions. The proof that reality exists, for example, will always seem to some people just silly intellectual gymnastics: they know that reality exists because they feel they are experiencing it, which is good enough. In terms of everyday life, of course, it *is* good enough. Philosophically, however, this position simply reflects our preconceptions and the limitations of our knowledge.

So, in what way is the application of philosophy important in the modern world? In jurisprudence, personal rights and responsibilities and the security of knowledge are important, as are ethics and the relationships between individuals in law-making. Ethical questions are ever more frequently asked in science and medicine. If neurology shows, as it well might, that what we think of as free will is not so free after all, it will have implications for how we should deal with crime. And attitudes towards God – whether we believe in one, whether He differs from the God or gods who others believe in – still cause wars and violence around the world.

Even in our day-to-day dealings with other people, an engagement with philosophy can lead us to a more thoughtful position. What rights and responsibilities do we feel we have in our relationships with partners, parents and children? Which choices are we free to make?

For every individual, the question of how to spend our lives, of which pursuits are worthwhile for the good of ourselves and others, is one that must be asked – we all seek Kierkegaard's 'idea for which I can live and die'. The answers will differ, but that doesn't matter.

Philosophy need not be some lofty and inaccessible discipline. Richard Rorty was sceptical about many of the more esoteric and abstruse philosophical arguments, saying that there are no *a priori* philosophical truths to be discovered. He felt that society would do better to learn about humankind and morality from novels than from philosophers, and maintained that the traditional form of philosophy has outlived its usefulness. Of course, this approach invited a flood of criticism from other professional philosophers, and he was accused of abandoning philosophy, even becoming an anti-philosopher. Like Jacques Derrida, he sawed through the branch he was sitting on – but from the opposite end of it.

Bertrand Russell spent most of his career – as a philosopher, logician, mathematician, historian, essayist, writer, social critic and political activist – working on logic and mathematics. In his later days he became more concerned with ethics and politics, but denied that this was the work of a philosopher:

> *'On these questions I did not write in my capacity as a philosopher; I wrote as a human being who suffered from the state of the world, wished to find some way of improving it, and was anxious to speak in plain terms to others who had similar feelings.'*

Obviously there is no more valuable use to which philosophy can be put than that.

Index